STUART PATERSON

Stuart Paterson's children's plays, first performed at Glasgow Citizens' Theatre, Edinburgh Royal Lyceum, Dundee Repertory Theatre, Newcastle Playhouse and Birmingham Old Rep, have since been staged throughout the UK, and also in Holland, Norway, Sweden and Finland. They include *Merlin the Magnificent, Beauty and the Beast*, *Cinderella*, *Granny and the Gorilla*, *The Sleeping Beauty*, *Hansel and Gretel*, *Puss in Boots*, the one-act play *The Secret Voice*, and adaptations of Hans Christian Andersen's *The Snow Queen*, George MacDonald's *The Princess and the Goblin*, Roald Dahl's *George's Marvellous Medicine*, J.M. Barrie's *Peter Pan*, Rudyard Kipling's *The Jungle Book*, and Michael Morpurgo's *Kensuke's Kingdom*. *Hansel and Gretel* and *Kensuke's Kingdom* were both nominated for the Barclay's Best Children's Play of the Year Award.

He has written *King of the Fields* for the Traverse Theatre, and new versions of Chekhov's *The Cherry Orchard*, *Uncle Vanya* and *The Seagull*. For the Scottish Youth Theatre he has written *In Traction* (later televised by the BBC) and adapted Zola's *Germinal*. He has also adapted Zola's *Thérèse Raquin* for Communicado Theatre Company, which was later staged at Newcastle Playhouse where his adaptation of William Trevor's *The Ballroom of Romance* was also produced. He has recently completed a new version of *Comrades* by August Strindberg, a new play, *Moon Street*, and a children's book, *Silversand*.

Television credits include *The Old Course* and the film *Workhorses*, which won the BBC Pharic McLaren Award for best script and best production. The short film *Somebody's Wee Nobody* won the Gold Award at the Chicago International Film Festival. Other film projects include original screenplays *The Pretender*, *Whisky Mac*, *Under the Same Moon* and screen adaptations of *The Kelpie's Pearls* by Mollie Hunter, *Fergus Lamont* by Robin Jenkins, and *Scandal* by Shusaku Endo.

Stuart has also written *Misterstourworm* and a short-story version of his play of *Hansel and Gretel* as compositions by Savourna Stevens

Other Adaptations in this Series

TREASURE ISLAND

adapted from Robert Louis Stevenson's novel by

Stuart Paterson

NICK HERN BOOKS

London

www.nickhernbooks.co.uk

A Nick Hern Book

This adaptation of *Treasure Island* first published in Great Britain in 2007 as a paperback original by Nick Hern Books Limited, 14 Larden Road, London W3 7ST

Reprinted 2008, 2012

Adaptation copyright © 2007 Stuart Paterson
Production Notes copyright © 2007 Stuart Paterson

Stuart Paterson has asserted his right to be identified as the author of this work

Cover image: feastcreative.com
Cover design: Ned Hoste, 2H

Typeset by Nick Hern Books, London
Printed in the UK by Mimeo Ltd, Huntingdon, Cambridgeshire PE29 6XX

A CIP catalogue record for this book is available from the British Library

ISBN 978 1 85459 590 4

Woodland
CARBON
www.woodlandcarbon.co.uk
NICK HERN BOOKS
Printed on Carbon Captured paper

Production Notes

by Stuart Paterson

Robert Louis Stevenson (1850-1894)

Born in Edinburgh, Stevenson's father was engineer to the Board of
Northern Lighthouses, and as a teenager Stevenson was sent to visit lighthouse construction sites around Scotland. He studied engineering at Edinburgh University, but soon abandoned it for the law, graduating as an
advocate in 1875. He had no real interest in pursuing law as a profession.
Writing was already his passion, stories and articles having been published in the *Edinburgh University Magazine* and the *Portfolio*.

Stevenson had been a sickly child and as a young man he began to suffer
from weak lungs, a condition which would plague him throughout his life.
A succession of doctors remained puzzled, never diagnosing tuberculosis.
Stevenson was tall and stick-thin, never weighing more than nine stone,
and never seen without a cigarette in his mouth.

His weak lungs led him to take frequent journeys abroad for the sake of
his health. These journeys were always paid for by his father, and some
believed his claims of ill-health were often just a ruse to put off making a
sensible career choice, and to get money for exotic jaunts. Certainly,
despite his frail health, Stevenson displayed great stamina, vigour and
courage on his travels. His *Inland Journey* (1878) describing a canoe tour
in Belgium and France, and his *Travels with a Donkey in the Cévennes*
(1879) earned him a small reputation as a travel writer. In 1879 he trav-
elled to California, living for a while in a gold-rush town. He married Mrs
Fanny Osbourne in 1880. After their stay at Calistoga, recorded in *The
Silverado Squatters* (1883), he returned to Britain.

Treasure Island, written between bouts of ill-health to entertain his bored
stepson, was published in 1883. Stevenson didn't set much store by it,
having to force himself to complete it as it was by then being serialised in
an unprestigious children's journal. Yet in *Treasure Island*, Stevenson
took the weary, predictable conventions of boys' adventure stories and
made them fresh, dark and utterly his own. The book's huge success took
him completely by surprise, and made him famous.

This success was followed by *The Strange Case of Dr Jekyll and Mr
Hyde* (1886), *Kidnapped* (1886), *Catriona*, its sequel (1893), *The Black
Arrow* (1888), *The Master of Ballantrae* (1889), and the unfinished *Weir
of Hermiston* (1896). He also wrote, as well as a great number of remark-
able poems, many short stories and novellas, including *The Beach of
Falesa*, *The Bottle Imp*, *The Dynamiter* and *Thrawn Janet*.

Increasingly, he came to find the literary world petty and stifling and, in
1888, he turned his back on it, setting out with his family for the South
Seas. He bought his house 'Valima' in Samoa where, for a few years, he
enjoyed good health. In 1894 he died suddenly from a ruptured blood
vessel in his brain.

The Samoans named him Tusitalla, 'The Teller of Tales'.

Adapting the Novel

I'll try to account for my adaptation of *Treasure Island*, and make some suggestions for how to stage it. Please take what you like from these notes which are not intended to be in any way prescriptive.

Although I've used them myself in the past, I've grown to dislike onstage narrators. I've seen too much of them and, even when they're used cleverly, with the narration often divided amongst the cast, it feels flat and undramatic – too much like the easy option it is. It just makes me want to go to the bar, or read the book, or read the book in the bar.

So, there's no narrator here – just Stevenson's fabulous action. This may mean, particularly in the voyage to the island, that time can feel very compressed, but I hope that can be accommodated by imaginative staging, and by an audience surrendering to the momentum of Stevenson's tale.

Yet action and momentum remain huge problems in adapting and staging this great book – not with regard to ships or voyages or fights or islands which can all be achieved – but rather in regard to the book's hurtling adventure. Its sheer pace risks leaving an audience breathless and uncaring.

I've seen a number of well-acted and impressively designed stage productions of *Treasure Island* but none of these versions, I felt, kept the audience emotionally engaged with the story. Jim Hawkins would bravely leap one fence after the other, leaving any emotional interest in him or his story further behind with every leap, until he would kill Israel Hands as easily as he might catch and kill a fish. I think there may be a golden rule here that states – if the central character kills someone, the audience has to care about it. And then Silver would find his freedom at the end – a freedom that Stevenson understood we all yearn for him to find, despite his crimes – yet he finds it not because a character in the play would set him free, for reasons we understand and care about, but because Stevenson allows him to walk free in the book. What works perfectly well in a book often sits very uncomfortably onstage, and that is when the playwright must look doubly hard to find a genuinely dramatic equivalent to described action.

Here are some of the ways my adaptation tries to find dramatic equivalents, and keep an audience emotionally engaged in both character and action:

• Jim's mother does not appear, partly because it would be wasteful to have an actress appear so briefly, never to appear again but, more importantly, to make Jim seem all the more alone and vulnerable. For the same reason, I've cut any reference to Jim's ill and dying father. If we think of anyone in the play as Jim's father, or father-figure, it needs to be Long John Silver.

• I haven't used Billy Bones' early warning to Jim to 'beware a one-legged man'. Many in an audience, especially children, may not know the book, and I wanted them to discover Silver's treachery at exactly the same moment Jim does, when he's hiding in the apple barrel.

• Captain Smollett describes Jim accurately as a 'noticing-lad' (he's not just bright – all his senses must be open to the world), and Silver too is highly perceptive. Just because Silver's a flatterer and a cunning dissembler doesn't mean there's not at least some sincerity in his smooth-talking first lines to Jim: 'You're young, you are, but as smart as paint. I seen that soon as I set eyes on you, and I'll talk to you like any man.' He will have noticed how firmly Jim has just stood up to George Merry ('I won't, sir'), and it's important to establish that, even as he's manipulating Jim not to tell of Black Dog being in his tavern, he nevertheless likes the boy from the start. There should be no doubt, without ever getting sentimental, that Jim reminds Silver of his young self, of his lost innocence and self-worth. I believe he's aware of that lost innocence even as he inadvertently gives himself away at the apple barrel by so casually repeating his first lines to Jim word for word to Dick Johnson. I'm sure that Silver, for all his charm and easy duplicity, carries a dark and self-lacerating view of his own character. He's too clever not to see through himself. That's why he's so fascinating.

• Jim Hawkins, as his name suggests, is every inch the brave, young hero, but it's crucial that he's not merely played as a swashbuckler. I've compressed some lines from the book and given them to Jim: 'Am I dreaming, John Silver? Am I really going to sea, to the open sea with a crew of pig-tailed seamen in a sweet ship called the *Hispaniola*?' His senses are truly and fully open to all that's around him, just as an actor's ought to be. And Silver's apparently brusque reply is preceded by the stage direction 'Moved by Jim's innocence'. He masks his emotions from Jim, but an audience needs to see them.

• I've given Jim a fear of climbing the mainmast, a fear that does not feature at all in the book. I hope that giving Jim a 'weakness' will make him seem even more human and believable and, besides, courage always seems more admirable when fear must be conquered first. It also gives Israel Hands something to torment him with, and, given that Jim will go on to kill Israel, I felt the play had to make much more of their antagonism. I also wanted to create a moment where Silver displays real kindness to Jim, so it's important to feel genuine goodness in Silver when he tells Jim: 'Ain't no reason for shame . . . Some can climb, and some can't, and there's an end to it.' And he then introduces Jim to his parrot – not for show, but to take Jim's mind off his feelings of shame. In Stevenson's novel this section comes to an end with the parrot uttering an unspecified swear-word. I couldn't come up with an oath chilling enough, or acceptable enough with children in the audience, and I've tried to carry out what I understand to be Stevenson's intention by having the parrot repeat instead: 'Cut his throat, drink his blood.' This leads on to one of Stevenson's masterstrokes. Silver explains the parrot's words by saying wryly 'You can't touch pitch, and not be mucked.' It should be clear that Silver's not talking about the parrot, he's talking about himself.

• I should make it clear that in the play, despite Livesey's warning at the end of the opening scene, Squire Trelawney has not 'blabbed' about the treasure, although he will have got drunk with Silver (maybe made drunk by Silver?), and therefore be unable to remember if he has talked or not. Silver skilfully suggests that Trelawney has spoken about the treasure when drunk in order to, at one stroke, explain away the crew's knowledge of it, and make himself seem honest and trustworthy in the eyes of Smollett, Trelawney and Livesey.

• At times I've given Jim something akin to a political/moral sensibility – and perhaps to a degree Silver too, when he replies angrily to Livesey and Trelawney: 'You've more greed for gold than any poor sailor I ever seen!' (I think at some deep level we all side with the pirates over the frockcoats.) But with Jim, this sensibility takes the form of a longing for justice, that youthful belief that the world can be made into a better place, that wrongs caused by man can be put right by man. And so he doesn't just run from the stockade to take back the ship; he runs because, as he says, 'We came here! We made it happen, no one else . . . Can't just wait here and watch people die one by one . . . That's just stupid . . . We started it, and we can end it . . . We can end it!' I needed to believe Jim had in him that young man's rage for justice, not only to bring credibility to his extraordinary daring, but also to make us care more about his actions as a character in a play.

• It's partly this sensibility that makes Jim defy Trelawney and hold true to his word to help Silver. He's made a promise, and I believe it's true to his character that he would stick to his word by letting Silver go free; it's far more than a simple matter of honour. There's buried love and yearning here too, and loss and regret at the passage of time and the ways of the world. In the play I wanted Silver to give voice to these conflicting emotions and, since there was nothing in the book for this, I looked instead to Stevenson's travel poems and gave Silver these amended lines from 'Sing Me a Song':

> *Sing me a song of a lad that is gone,*
> *Say could that lad be I?*
> *Merry of soul he sailed on a day*
> *Over the seas so high.*
> *Give me again all that was there,*
> *Give me the sun that shone.*
> *Give me the eyes, give me the soul,*
> *Give me the lad that's gone.*

Character Descriptions

JIM HAWKINS   A fifteen-year-old boy. Imaginative, brave and good-hearted, but a part of him is alive to the darkness around him, and troubled by it. He's not just a swashbuckling hero. The events of the story test him to the limits.

BILLY BONES   A booze-raddled old buccaneer, a killer who would slit your throat as soon as look at you, but he's not without charm. Despite Bones' brutality, Jim has a grudging affection for him because he understands that, beneath the swagger, he's old and ill and alone.

SQUIRE TRELAWNEY   A country squire who funds the voyage as a rich man's jaunt. Likeable in many ways, if a little pompous and self-regarding, but I suspect we come to like him less and less, and regret that he gets the gold, especially when he's rich enough without it. He's not a coward though, and seems to feel some regret for the carnage let loose by his quest.

LONG JOHN SILVER   One-legged, so the actor may need to be fit and agile (see separate note about his peg-leg). A mesmerising, magical man of contrast and ambiguity. Handsome, charismatic, brave, a natural leader of men, and every young boy's dream uncle. But he's also a liar, a schemer and a ruthless killer. Once again, Stevenson cherishes and explores ambiguity, and at the end of the play, despite all his duplicity and savagery, we should nonetheless feel a strong and troubled regard for him, a kind of buried mourning for the great man he could never quite become.

CAPTAIN SMOLLETT   An experienced sea-captain, dour and a stickler, but his courage and good sense become more appealing and important as the danger intensifies.

BLACK DOG   A killer, but you wouldn't see it coming because he'd knife you in the back.

ISRAEL HANDS   A fantastically skilled sailor, particularly in the rigging, but he's arrogant and sadistic. When Jim kills him, the whole audience should feel a sense of relief.

MORGAN   A cut-throat, mean and vicious.

BLIND PEW   Like a terrifying creature from a nightmare – blinded, driven, merciless.

MR ARROW   A good, honest first mate who pays with his life for his honesty.

TOM   A decent old sea-dog with the courage to defy Silver.

BEN GUNN   A lively, sparky, almost magical man, driven wild and strange from his years spent marooned on the island. We like and trust him though, and he provides hope, and relief from the violence all around him.

DOCTOR LIVESEY   A bored country doctor up for adventure – and gold! On one level he's decent, trustworthy and a loyal friend to Jim, on another we may suspect him of greed and hypocrisy which makes him less conventional and more interesting.

JOHN   A decent young farmboy frightened away from the inn by Billy Bones.

DICK JOHNSTON   A young sailor led astray by Silver and the pirates.

HARRY   A brave farmworker who challenges Billy Bones' bullish swagger, and who has enough sense to back down.

GEORGE MERRY   An ambitious pirate who dreams of usurping Silver. Clever and dangerous, he's nevertheless no match for Silver.

ABRAHAM GRAY   A good-hearted, brave and experienced sailor who remains loyal to his captain, and pays with his life.

JOB ANDERSON   A vicious cut-throat.

Casting

This adaptation can be performed with a cast of ten, with the following doubling:

JIM HAWKINS
BILLY BONES/CAPTAIN SMOLLETT
BLACK DOG/ISRAEL HANDS/MORGAN
BLIND PEW/MR ARROW/TOM/BEN GUNN
DOCTOR LIVESEY
SQUIRE TRELAWNEY
LONG JOHN SILVER
DICK JOHNSON/JOHN
GEORGE MERRY/HARRY
JOB ANDERSON/ABRAHAM GRAY

The actors playing DICK JOHNSON, GEORGE MERRY and JOB ANDERSON can also play the REVENUE OFFICERS, unnamed PIRATES and SAILORS who rob the inn, drink in Silver's tavern, and crew the *Hispaniola*.

Obviously it would also be possible for every character to be played by a different actor, so this adaptation allows for a cast of nineteen actors with speaking roles, plus as many unspeaking performers as you wish.

Although all the characters are male, in a school or youth group production, some or all of the characters may be played by girls.

Set and Design

To *suggest* the world of *Treasure Island* is likely to be far more effective than faithful and expensive realism. I've expressed that view in some of the stage directions, most notably in this description of the ship: *'Some or all of the most magical components may be there – the figurehead, the bridge and wheel, the captain's window, the galley and stove, the mast and rigging soaring into the air – but they suggest the grace and mystery of a ship rather than represent too faithfully its reality.'*

For the original production of this adaptation, Jackie Trousdale's design – all rope-ladder rigging and open decking – worked equally well for an inn, ship or stockade. A mast made up of what may be coiling vines or wound rope suggested tree and island jungle as well as a soaring mainmast, its ragged sail like a magical cloud. With great simplicity and style, her design brought to life the whole world of the book in a way that looked and felt like a young boy's dream of adventure.

Fights

Obviously the more thrilling the fights, skirmishes and shoot-outs are, the better – as long as the actors are safe. In general, short, sharp and carefully rehearsed fights tend to have greater impact than overextended sequences.

Some Ideas for Staging

Long John Silver's peg-leg

As I was adapting the novel, I found myself worrying about the physical demands a wooden peg-leg would make on the actor playing Long John Silver. I kept putting these worries to the back of my mind, telling myself that a peg-leg was a given, iconic part of his character and there was nothing I could do about it. But then I began to imagine him with a false leg as opposed to a wooden peg, and the greater freedom and comfort that this might bring, and this is the note I sent to Neal Foster of Birmingham Stage Company:

'A hollow casing or artificial leg may allow the actor playing Silver to stand on both legs, considerably easing the physical burden of playing him on one leg. He should still have a crutch as he uses this so effectively as a weapon, and a strange, loping walk, as this makes him so distinctive and sinister. There also still needs to be the sense of it being impossible for Silver to get up from the ground without help or something to hold onto. The only problem with an artificial leg would be if it makes him too mobile in a conventional sense, too much like an ordinary man. One of Silver's most impressive traits is how he copes so well and uncomplainingly with his missing leg.

An artificial leg could and should look great, probably visible from the knee down only, as if he's proud of it, certainly not ashamed. If we can imagine ourselves in Silver's world he would have known all kinds of ship's carpenters, barrel-makers and blacksmiths, and they all would have both liked and feared him. Perhaps any casing they would have made for Silver might reflect this duality: rough and ready, but also strangely beautiful, perhaps carved, a little like a pirate's totem pole. It could also perhaps have a golden band around it, and if it were made of wood and black metal, it could have something powerful and chilling about it; a power reminiscent of the devil's cloven foot. The idea of a hooved bottom plate would fit a world of blacksmiths and coopers, but also give Silver a memorably diabolic presence, something that Stevenson, I think, would have enjoyed.

It may be that in the end a conventional peg is best, but it's worth thinking this through for the sake of the actor.'

Imaginative solutions to difficult problems are often the most memorable and rewarding elements of any theatre production.

Long John Silver's parrot

The parrot could be real, if there is time and money available, and the ability and willingness to take care of it properly. It is, however, most likely to be a puppet, operated by hand or remote control. If it's working well, without ever becoming too much of a distraction, then Silver can have it with him whenever he feels comfortable with it.

For Isy

This adaptation of *Treasure Island* was first performed by
Birmingham Stage Company at Birmingham Old Rep on 14
November 2007, before a national tour. The cast was as follows:

JIM HAWKINS	Iain Ridley
LONG JOHN SILVER	Gavin Robertson
BILLY BONES/	
CAPTAIN SMOLLETT	Nigel Harris
BLACK DOG/ISRAEL HANDS	Brendan Foster
BLIND PEW/BEN GUNN	Christopher Llewellyn
DOCTOR LIVESEY	Anthony Houghton
SQUIRE TRELAWNEY	Leo Atkin
DICK JOHNSON	Graeme Dalling
GEORGE MERRY	Matthew Weyland
JOB ANDERSON/GRAY	Lawrence Stubbings

Director   Greg Banks
Designer   Jackie Trousdale
Lighting Designer   Jason Taylor
Sound Designer   Tom Lishman
Music   Matthew Scott
Company Stage Manager   Adrian Littlejohns
Deputy Stage Manager   Sara Crathorne

Characters

BILLY BONES
HARRY
JOHN
JIM HAWKINS
BLACK DOG
BLIND PEW
DOCTOR LIVESEY
SQUIRE TRELAWNEY
LONG JOHN SILVER
CAPTAIN SMOLLETT
MR ARROW
ISRAEL HANDS
DICK
TOM
BEN GUNN
ABRAHAM GRAY
JOB ANDERSON
MORGAN
GEORGE MERRY

PIRATES, SAILORS, DRINKERS, REVENUE OFFICERS

This text went to press before the end of rehearsals and may differ slightly from the play as performed.

ACT ONE

Scene One

The year 17—. Evening. The Admiral Benbow Inn and the shadowy road outside.

Two locals, HARRY *and* JOHN, *drink together. A sturdy old sea dog (the* CAP'N*) drinks alone at a table. His tarry pigtail falls over the shoulder of his soiled blue coat. His face is marked by the livid scar of a sabre cut along one cheek. He half-sings and mutters quietly to himself.*

CAP'N.
> Fifteen men on the dead man's chest –
> Yo-ho-ho and a bottle of rum!
> Drink and the Devil have done for the rest,
> Yo-ho-ho and a bottle of . . .

He slams down his tankard, and calls out roughly.

Rum!

HARRY *looks daggers at the* CAP'N *who picks up on the challenge in a flash.*

What are you lookin' at, you dog? You, aye, you, I'm talking to you!

Luckily for HARRY, JIM HAWKINS *enters, a fifteen-year-old boy who is working in his mother's inn.*

Move your bones, boy! Where's your mother?

JIM. Gone to look after Aunt Meg . . .

CAP'N. And I says she should be looking after me! Rum!

JIM. You haven't paid this month's lodgings.

CAP'N. No backchat, or by thunder you'll be sorry!

JOHN. Pay the boy.

HARRY. Aye, pay up or go!

CAP'N. I don't recollec' askin' either o' you gentlemen your opinion.

JIM. It's all right, Harry . . . (*Filling a jug with rum, to the* CAP'N.) You should remember what Doctor Livesey told you – 'No more rum if you want to live.'

CAP'N. All doctors is swabs! I've sailed with the wickedest men God ever allowed on the sea, so why should the Cap'n fear a doctor?

JIM has come to his table and is pouring a drink. The CAP'N *seizes the jug, drinks gratefully from his tankard, and pours himself another. JIM turns away from him, and suddenly the ruined old buccaneer seems very alone. He speaks with a hint of wheedling apology, as if he needs JIM's good opinion.*

The name of rum for me may be death, but I needs it, hear me, I needs it . . . You'll be paid, boy, don't you worry . . . You be good to this old dog, and one day maybe you'll be richer than the Devil himself . . . Just you keep a weather-eye open for any seafaring men . . .

He stands and takes up his brass telescope.

Time to take my turn along the cliff . . .

HARRY. Why do you watch for ships, morning, noon and . . .

CAP'N (*icily hard*). Never ask why or what to the Cap'n! Do you hear me, farmboy?

HARRY *squares up to the* CAP'N.

JOHN (*quietly, urging his friend to back down*). Harry . . .

CAP'N. Well?

HARRY (*saying the words, but defiant still*). I hear you.

CAP'N. Now, Jim, if anyone comes lookin' for me, you let me know quick as lightnin' . . . And when I comes back I'll expect food on the table . . . (*Pulls out a knife in a blur of movement, holds it to* HARRY's *throat*.) And if you're still here when I comes back then we'll finish our little talk. I'll look forward to it.

He goes, singing and muttering to himself, as if nothing untoward has happened.

Fifteen men on the dead man's chest,
Yo-ho-ho and a bottle of rum,
Drink and the Devil have done for the rest . . .

HARRY *prepares to leave.*

JIM. I'm sorry, Harry . . .

HARRY. We're sorry too, Jim . . . (*Finishes his drink.*)

JOHN. We can't drink here . . . Not with that old pig.

HARRY. We'll be back when you're rid of him.

A stranger (BLACK DOG) *slips silently into the inn. He's a pale, tallowy creature, missing two fingers on his left hand, and carrying a cutlass in his belt.*

JOHN. Give our best to your mother.

JIM. I will.

HARRY. Goodnight, then.

JIM. Goodnight.

HARRY and JOHN *go.* JIM *lays the* CAP'N*'s table.* BLACK DOG *watches him.*

BLACK DOG. Come here, sonny. Come nearer . . . Is this here table for my mate Bill?

JIM. No, it's for a man staying in our inn. We call him the Captain.

BLACK DOG. Well, my mate Bill would be called the Captain, as like as not. He has a cut on one cheek, has my mate Bill. We'll put it for argument like, that your Captain has a cut on one cheek – and we'll put it, if you like, that that cheek's the right one. (JIM *can't help but nod.*) Ah, well, there we are! Is my mate Bill in this here house?

JIM. He's out walking.

BLACK DOG. Which way, sonny? Show me. (*Dragging* JIM *with him, he peers outside.*) Here he is now, with a spyglass under his arm, bless his 'art. (*Holds* JIM *roughly, speaks in a way that is half-fawning and half-sneering.*) I've a son of my own, as like you as two blocks, but the great thing for boys is to do what they're told. So you an' me'll just wait back here, and we'll give Bill a little surprise, that's what we'll do.

He pulls JIM *into hiding, loosens his cutlass. Enter the* CAP'N, *striding to his table, looking forward to his meal.*

CAP'N. I'm a plain man. Rum and bacon and egg is all I want.

BLACK DOG. Bill . . . Billy Bones.

The CAP'N *spins round as if he's been called by a ghost or the Devil, and gasps the stranger's name.*

BILLY BONES. Black Dog!

BLACK DOG (*emboldened by* BILLY BONES'*fear*). And who else? Black Dog as ever was, come to see his old shipmate at The Admiral Benbow Inn . . . Ah, Bill, we've seen a sight of times, us two, since I lost them two talons. (*Holds up his ravaged hand.*)

BILLY BONES. You've run me down, all right, so here I am. Speak up! Speak and be done!

BLACK DOG. I'll have a glass of rum from this dear child, as I've took such a liking to . . . And we'll sit down and talk square, like old shipmates.

BILLY BONES. No, we won't be doing that. What's mine's mine, and you'll be having none of it! You can swing for it, you dog!

They pull their cutlasses and fall to, exchanging slashing, murderous strokes. It's clear from their brutal skill that they've killed many times before. BILLY*'s strength begins to tell, and* BLACK DOG *retreats.*

BLACK DOG. Aye, but we've found you, Billy Bones! We've found you now! (*He flees the inn.*)

BILLY *stands for a few moments as if in a dream, passing his hands over his eyes several times.*

BILLY BONES. Rum . . . (*But he staggers, and has to hold onto a wall to stay standing.*)

JIM. Are you hurt?

BILLY BONES. I must get away from here . . . Rum . . . (*He falls, slumps against the table.*)

JIM (*passing him his tankard*). You're not well . . . You need to rest.

BILLY BONES (*drinks gratefully*). Can't rest! They'll have the Black Spot on me! But I'll do them yet . . . All Flint's crew, all of them that's left . . . (*He tries to stand, but sways dizzily.*) My ears is ringing . . . Lay me back. (JIM *helps him back down against the table. He speaks dreamily, as if something has finally unwound within him.*) It's my old sea-chest they're after . . . I was Cap'n Flint's first mate, I was, and I'm the only one as knows the place . . . He gave it to me in Savannah when he lay a-dyin' . . . Are you there, lad?

JIM. I'm here.

BILLY BONES. You're the only one's been good to me . . . Maybe I'll share with you equals, but they won't have it . . .

He continues to rave and mutter to himself. A sinister tap-tapping sound begins, and grows steadily louder. BILLY BONES *clutches his head and moans, as if the sound echoes in his head.*

Sounds in my head . . . Like grasshoppers . . .

JIM. No . . . It's coming from outside . . . (*He steps outside, calls out.*) Who's there? Hullo . . . Who's there?

He starts back in fear when a blind beggar (BLIND PEW), *tapping with his stick, emerges from the misty road. He's a dreadful figure, hunched, with a ragged shade over his eyes, and wearing a huge, tattered sea-cloak with a hood. He stops and addresses the air in front of him in an odd, sing-song voice.*

BLIND PEW. Will any kind friend inform a poor blind man who has lost the sight of his eyes in the gracious defence of his country, England, and God bless King George – where or what part of this country he may now be?

JIM. Black Hill Cove. The Admiral Benbow Inn.

BLIND PEW. I hear a voice, a young voice. Will you give me your hand, my kind young friend, and lead me in?

JIM *holds out his hand and the horrible creature grips him like a vice.*

Now, boy, take me in to the Captain!

JIM. No, sir, I will not!

BLIND PEW. Take me in or I'll break your arm! Lead me straight to him, and when he's near, cry out, 'Here's a friend for you, Bill.' If you don't . . . (*Twists his arm viciously.*) Come now, march!

They go inside.

JIM (*in a trembling voice*). Here's a friend for you, Bill.

BILLY BONES *looks up in terror and mortal sickness.*

BILLY BONES. Pew . . . Blind Pew . . .

He makes a movement to rise, but he lacks the strength and will.

BLIND PEW. Now, Bill, sit where you are. If I can't see, I can hear a finger stirring. Business is business. Hold out your left hand. Boy, take his left hand by the wrist, and bring it near to my right.

As if caught in some nightmare, BILLY BONES *and* JIM *both obey.* BLIND PEW *passes something into* BILLY*'s hand which closes instantly around it.*

(*With cruel satisfaction.*) There now, it's done.

He lets go of JIM *and leaves the inn with almost supernatural nimbleness, the sound of his stick tap-tapping into the distance.* BILLY BONES *summons the courage to open his hand. He sees what he most dreads.*

BILLY BONES. The Black Spot! They means to kill me. (*Reads the back of the Black Spot.*) The stroke of six, it says, that's when they'll come for me . . . By thunder, we'll do 'em yet! My chest, bring me my chest! Hurry! (JIM *pulls out a battered old sea-chest from its place of hiding.*) The key, take the key and open it! (*He takes a key from a length of string around his neck, and gives it to* JIM, *who unlocks and opens the sea-chest.*) The treasure wrapped in oilcloth . . . Hurry, lad . . . Find it . . . Find it quick . . .

JIM *rummages through the chest pulling out clothes, a quadrant, sticks of tobacco, bags of coins, an ornate pistol, brass compasses and some West Indian seashells – memorials of a wandering life at sea.*

JIM. I can't see any oilcloth.

BILLY BONES. There's not one o' them could take me on . . . Or maybe there was one, aye, but only one . . . It's mine by rights, hear me! We'll do 'em yet, and we'll be rich, lad, richer than the Devil . . . We'll do 'em yet . . . (*Falls silent, dies.*)

JIM *lifts out a small bundle wrapped in oilcloth.*

JIM. Is this it? Is this what you want? Cap'n . . . Cap'n? (*Draws back in horror.*) Dead . . . He's dead . . . (*The clock strikes six.*) The stroke of six! The time on the Black Spot . . . I won't stay here! (*He goes to run outside but he's prevented by sounds from outside.*) They're here!

JIM *flings himself down, hiding in desperation, just as the door is smashed open.* BLACK DOG *and* BLIND PEW *rush in, followed by a gang of* CUT-THROATS.

BLIND PEW. In, you dogs, in, in!

BLACK DOG. Bill's dead.

BLIND PEW. Search him! Find the chest!

BLACK DOG. The chest's here. It's open!

BLIND PEW. Is it there? (*In a frenzy.*) Tell me quick, is it there?

BLACK DOG *searches, as the* CUT-THROATS *pocket what they can of the strewn contents of the chest.*

BLACK DOG. Don't see it here, no-how.

BLIND PEW. Is it on Bill? My soul, if I had eyes!

They quickly search BILLY BONES' *pockets.*

BLACK DOG. There's nothing!

BLIND PEW. It's that boy! I wish I'd put his eyes out! He was here no time ago. Scatter, lads, and find him! Rout the house out!

Just as JIM *must be discovered, a whistle is heard from outside.*

BLACK DOG. Dirk's whistle! (*They listen. The whistle is heard again.*) Twice! That's our signal! We'll have to budge, mates.

BLIND PEW. Dirk was a fool and a coward from the first! It's here someplace and we'd be rich as kings if we could find it! There wasn't one of you dared face Bill, but I did it, a blind man!

A whistle is heard again from outside, followed by the sound in the distance of horses galloping.

BLACK DOG. Hang it, Pew, don't stand here squalling!

BLACK DOG *and the* CUT-THROATS *flee the inn.*

BLIND PEW (*in a frenzy of indignation*). Am I to lose my chance because of you? Am I to be a poor, crawling beggar sponging for rum when I might be rolling in a coach? (*He senses that he's alone. He goes outside, calls pitifully as the approaching horses grow louder.*) Johnny, Black Dog, Dirk, you won't leave old Pew, mates, not old Pew!

He steps blindly into the darkness, and falls to his death under the thundering hooves.

Enter DOCTOR LIVESEY *and* SQUIRE TRELAWNEY *followed by some* REVENUE OFFICERS.

TRELAWNEY. He stepped right in front of us. He's dead, stone dead.

JIM. In there, Doctor, the Cap'n too . . .

LIVESEY *goes in and examines the body of* BILLY BONES, *before signalling to the* REVENUE OFFICERS *to take it away.*

TRELAWNEY. There was a strange lugger moored off Kitt's Point. A gang of them came ashore. We followed as fast as we could.

JIM. Lucky you did, sir.

LIVESEY (*coming back out*). What were they after? Money, I suppose, or rum.

JIM. Not money, I think it was this. (*By a kind of* droit de seigneur, *he offers the oilskin package to* TRELAWNEY.) I think you should have it, Squire Trelawney.

TRELAWNEY. Away with you, boy. It's yours by right, and yours to open. Get on with it!

JIM (*unwrapping the package*). The Cap'n told me . . . Said he was given it by a Captain Flint.

TRELAWNEY. The bloodthirstiest pirate that ever lived! Blackbeard was but a child to Flint. (*He signals for a lamp to be brought.*)

LIVESEY. But the point is, had he money? Supposing we were to find some clue to where Flint hid his treasure, would that treasure amount to much?

TRELAWNEY. Amount, sir! It will amount to this – I'll fit out a ship in Bristol Dock, I'll take you and Hawkins, and I'll have the treasure if I search a year!

A REVENUE OFFICER *brings an oil lamp to* TRELAWNEY, *and under its magical light* JIM *spreads out a map on the ground.* LIVESEY *and* TRELAWNEY *crouch beside him.*

JIM. It's the map of an island!

TRELAWNEY. Nine miles long, and five miles across.

JIM. It's shaped like a dragon standing with a hill in the middle marked 'Spyglass'.

LIVESEY. There are three crosses marked in red ink. Two in the north, look, and one in the south-west, and next to it is written . . .

TRELAWNEY. By my soul!

JIM. 'Treasure' . . . It says treasure! It's a treasure map!

TRELAWNEY. Tomorrow I start for Bristol! In three weeks, two weeks, no ten days, we'll have the best ship and choicest crew in England! Hawkins will be cabin boy – I'll speak to your mother, send one of my maids to help with the inn – and you, Livesey, you'll be ship's doctor. I am Admiral!

LIVESEY. I'll go with you, and so will Jim. There's only one man I'm afraid of.

TRELAWNEY. Who, sir? Name the dog!

LIVESEY. You, sir, for you cannot hold your tongue. We are not the only ones who know of this chart . . . Those fellows who attacked the inn, and more, I dare say, not far off . . .

TRELAWNEY. Livesey, you are always in the right of it. I'll be as silent as the grave.

JIM. Will you keep this safe, Doctor?

LIVESEY (*taking the map*). I will, Jim. Come then – to the sea and to glory!

ALL. To the sea and to glory!

Scene Two

The sound of seagulls. Bristol Docks – The Spyglass Tavern. Busy, loud, full of seafaring men. The tavern is ruled by its landlord, a tall, charismatic man with one leg – LONG JOHN SILVER. He manages his rough clients with easy charm and dexterity, able to move faster with his crutch than any two-legged man, and using his crutch like a weapon if he has to.

JIM *enters the noisy tavern, all the drinking and raised voices making him look and feel very young and vulnerable. He announces politely –*

JIM. A message for John Silver . . . (*No one pays the slightest atten-tion. He speaks more loudly.*) A message from Squire Trelawney for John Silver.

MERRY, *one of the seamen drinking in the tavern, takes excep-tion to* JIM'*s youthfulness and polite way of speaking.*

MERRY. Pipe down, you swab!

JIM. A message from . . .

MERRY. I said, stow the gab! (*Offers him rum.*) Here – this'll fix you.

JIM. No, thank you, sir.

MERRY (*seizing any opportunity to take offence*). What's the matter? Won't you drink with me?

JIM. I won't, sir.

MERRY *gets angrily to his feet, but* SILVER *comes between them.*

SILVER. Leave him be, George! (SILVER *pushes* MERRY *back down with his crutch. To* JIM.) You're young, you are, but as smart as paint. I seen that soon as I set eyes on you, and I'll talk to you like any man.

JIM. Are you John Silver, sir?

SILVER. I am, sir. And who may you be?

JIM. Jim Hawkins, cabin boy. (*They shake hands.*) Squire Trelawney asks you kindly to come aboard as ship's cook, and bring with you the men you found as crew. We sail on the morning tide.

A figure emerges from the crowd and makes to creep out of the tavern, but JIM *sees him and recognises him.*

It's him! It's Black Dog! Stop him!

JIM *rushes to block* BLACK DOG'*s escape, but* BLACK DOG *pulls a knife and lunges at* JIM. SILVER *trips him, but he gets to his feet and flees the inn.*

He robbed my mother's inn!

SILVER. I don't care two coppers who he is, he hasn't paid his score! Joseph, run and catch him!

One of the DRINKERS *by the door leaps up and goes in pursuit of* BLACK DOG.

Who did you say he was? Black what?

JIM. Dog, sir. Has Squire Trelawney not told you of the buccaneers? He was one of them.

SILVER. One of those swabs, was he? And in my house! (*To* MERRY.) You, there, was you drinkin' with that swab? (*Very sternly.*) Step up here. (MERRY *steps forward.*) Now, you never clapped eyes on that Black Dog before, did you?

MERRY. Not I, John, never.

SILVER. And you didn't know his name?

MERRY. No, sir.

SILVER. By the powers, it's as well for you! If you'd been mixed up with the like o' that, you'd never set foot in here again! Get back to your place, you lubber! (MERRY *obeys.*) Now, let's see . . . Black Dog? I don't know the name, yet I kind of think I've seen the swab. He used to come in here with a blind beggar. What was his name? Mew? Hew?

JIM (*excitedly*). Pew, Blind Pew!

SILVER. That was it, and a right shark he looked too! See here, now, Hawkins, what's the Squire to think if he hears I had that confounded dog drinking in my own house, and then let him slip right out from under my nose? It hurts my pride, it does, but what could I do with this old timber I hobble on? You won't tell the Squire, will you?

JIM. I will tell him only how you saved me from a cut-throat's knife.

SILVER. Much obliged. You've the makings of a cap'n about you, mark my words.

JIM. But we so nearly had him! Oh, I wish we'd caught him.

SILVER. He's gone and good riddance, I say. (*To the crowded bar.*) Come on, you swabs, let's put a smile on the lad's face. A trick, a trick! Hurry, now, shake a leg!

SILVER *ushers them quickly into their places, and they perform a ribald and mischievous ship's jape –* SAILOR 1 *fills a set of bellows from a tankard of ale.* SAILOR 2 *adopts the exaggerated posture of a 'fountain angel'.* SAILOR 1 *holds the bellows against* SAILOR 2*'s backside.* SAILOR 1 *works the bellows, a short delay, and a jet of ale shoots out of* SAILOR 2*'s mouth and is caught in a tankard by* SILVER *who bows to* JIM. *The trick surprises* JIM *into laughter – the first time we have seen him laugh.* SILVER *laughs along with him.*

A laugh, hurray and at last, a laugh! So, come then, Jim Hawkins, cabin boy. We've had our orders from the Squire. But it's the sea that's calling us. You can hear it, can't you? Right down deep inside.

JIM. I can hear it!

SILVER (*smiling, sharing his excitement*). Aye, and there's no sound like it. Time to put on my old cocked hat and step along. (*Calling out.*) The sea's calling! The sea's calling, and there's a ship waiting! Come, men, you know who you are. We sail on the morning tide!

> Come, now, you men o' the sea,
> Come, now, to the sea, and to me.

The MEN *answer his call and* SILVER *and his* CREW *rig and prepare the ship, and it takes shape in front of our eyes. Some or all of the most magical components may be there – the figurehead, the bridge and wheel, the captain's window, the galley and stove, the mast and rigging soaring into the air – but they suggest the grace and mystery of a ship rather than represent too faithfully its reality.*

Scene Three

The deck of the Hispaniola. CAPTAIN SMOLLETT, *a stern and capable seaman, paces angrily.* LIVESEY, TRELAWNEY, JIM *and* SILVER *stand in a group.* SQUIRE TRELAWNEY *now wears brand new, expensive sea-going clothes.* SMOLLETT *addresses the first mate,* MR ARROW.

SMOLLETT. Mr Arrow, please inform Squire Trelawney I wish to speak with him.

MR ARROW. Aye, sir.

He delivers his message, and TRELAWNEY *approaches* SMOLLETT.

TRELAWNEY. I am always at the Captain's orders. Well, Captain, all ready to sail I hope, all shipshape and seaworthy?

SMOLLETT. Better speak plain, I believe. I don't like the men, and I don't like this voyage.

TRELAWNEY (*angered*). Perhaps, sir, you don't like my ship.

SMOLLETT. I can't speak to that, not having seen her tried. The *Hispaniola* seems a clever craft, more I can't say.

TRELAWNEY. Then possibly, you don't like your employer!

LIVESEY. Stay, gentlemen, stay. The Captain has either said too much or too little. You say you don't like the men?

SMOLLETT. I don't like them, sir. I should have had the choosing of my own hands.

LIVESEY. Perhaps my friend should have sought your advice, but the offence, if there be one, was unintentional. And you don't like the voyage. Why, sir?

SMOLLETT. I was engaged under sealed orders to sail this ship. So far so good. And then I hear we're going after treasure, and I hear it from my own men! I don't like treasure voyages on any account, and I don't like them, above all, when they're secret and every manjack aboard knows the secret except the man who's paid to command the ship!

TRELAWNEY. I never said a word! Not to a soul!

SMOLLETT. Well, there's been too much blabbing!

LIVESEY (*who suspects* TRELAWNEY). Far too much.

TRELAWNEY (*mounting his defence*). Take this man! (*He pulls* SILVER *forward*.) Take this man! As able a seaman as ever there was, Long John Silver, who has lost a leg in his country's service. I was standing by the dock when, by the merest chance, I fell to talking with him. I thought I had found only a ship's cook, but in no time it was a crew I had found! You don't like the men? Why, sir, between Silver and myself, we got together a company of fellows of unbreakable spirit. By heaven, I believe we could fight a frigate! And then you talk of blabbing. (*To* SILVER.) Tell me, Silver, have you heard any word of treasure from these lips?

SILVER (*awkwardly*). I can't rightly say, sir.

TRELAWNEY. You will say, man! Did I speak of treasure or not?

SILVER. Now, sir, who's really talking when a man's had a drink or two? Is it the man himself, or some shadow who speaks? Who can say?

SMOLLETT (*almost cracking a smile*). I like your honesty, Silver.

TRELAWNEY (*distraught*). So I did blab! I'd never have believed it . . . Captain, gentlemen, you have my apology.

SILVER (*touching his forelock solemnly*). If I may speak, sir. The men we brought aboard, they've lived their whole lives with tales of treasure, and they makes nothing of them. They'll do their duty plain and simple, you have my word for that.

SMOLLETT. Well, Silver, I hope you cook as well as you talk. And you, boy, you can help Silver in his work.

JIM (*unable to hide his pleasure*). Oh yes, thank you, sir.

SMOLLETT. Then, on your way, and get some work! The hands will want fed!

JIM. Aye, sir.

JIM *goes with* SILVER.

SMOLLETT. I'll have no favourites on this ship.

LIVESEY (*to* SMOLLETT). So how may we heal matters with you, Captain?

SMOLLETT. They're putting the guns and powder in the fore-hold. There's a better place under my cabin. I say we put them there.

TRELAWNEY. Why? You fear a mutiny?

SMOLLETT. I am responsible for the ship's safety, and the life of every man aboard. I'm asking you to take certain precautions, or let me resign my berth, and there you have it.

TRELAWNEY. I have heard you, I will do as you desire, but I think the worse of you for it.

SMOLLETT. That's as you please, sir. You'll find I do my duty.

SMOLLETT *goes*.

LIVESEY. Well, Trelawney, I believe you've managed to get two honest men on board – that man, and John Silver.

TRELAWNEY. Silver, if you like, but as for Captain Smollett, I declare his conduct unmanly, unsailorly, and downright un-English!

ARROW. All hands to weigh anchor! Step along, now!

The CREW *man the capstan bars.*

GRAY. Come, Silver, tip us a song.

SILVER. Which one?

ISRAEL. The old one.

SILVER *sings as the* MEN *push the bars.*

SILVER.
Fifteen men on the dead man's chest –

The whole CREW *bear chorus.*

CREW.
Yo-ho-ho, and a bottle of rum!

SILVER.
Drink and the Devil have done for the rest –

CREW.
Yo-ho-ho and a bottle of rum!

On 'ho' they drive the bars before them with a will.

SILVER.
Fifteen men of the whole ship's list –

CREW.
Yo-ho-ho and a bottle of rum!

SILVER.
Dead and be damned and the rest gone whist –

CREW.
Yo-ho-ho and a bottle of rum!

As JIM *stands gazing up at the masts and rigging, a shiver runs down his spine. One of the* CREW, ISRAEL HANDS, *approaches him.*

ISRAEL. High, ain't it?

JIM. It goes up and up . . . To the clouds . . .

ISRAEL. Up there, see . . . That man looks small as a fly in a spider's web . . . Climb up, why don'tcha?

JIM. No, I couldn't . . .

ISRAEL. You ain't scared, is you?

ARROW. Don't stand idle, there!

ISRAEL. Aye, aye, sir.

ARROW. I know you, Israel Hands. I've sailed with you before this. I don't like you, hear me, and I don't trust you. I'll be keepin' my eye on you. (ISRAEL *eyes him challengingly*.) To work with you! (ISRAEL *obeys, but with an insolent smile. To* JIM.) Stay clear of that one, if you know what's good for you.

SMOLLETT. Mr Arrow, are we cast off and ready?

ARROW. Cast off and ready, sir!

SMOLLETT. Then hoist the mainsail.

ARROW. Hoist the mainsail!

The CREW *perform with discipline and precision*.

SMOLLETT. They may be ugly, but they know their work, by thunder! (*To* ARROW.) Set a course, south by south-west.

ARROW. South by south-west it is, sir!

SMOLLETT. Steady as she goes.

ARROW. Steady as she goes, sir!

JIM. Am I dreaming, John Silver? Am I really going to sea, to the open sea with a crew of pigtailed seamen in a sweet ship called the *Hispaniola*?

SILVER (*moved by* JIM*'s innocence*). You'll know it ain't no dream if we don't get grub ready, and right quick! Move along, there!

JIM *and* SILVER *prepare food, soon learning to work well together in the cramped space*. SILVER *carries his crutch by a lanyard around his neck to have both hands as free as possible. He has a line rigged to help him move easily and quickly.* JIM *watches him in amazement*.

JIM. Every day he gets faster. He's the quickest man aboard.

ISRAEL (*taking the chance to idle*). He's no common man. He can speak like a book when he wants. And brave – a lion's nothing alongside Long John Silver. I seen him grapple four, and knock their heads together, and him unarmed!

ARROW. I won't tell you again, Israel Hands! There's a blow coming. Get aloft, and strike the topsail!

ISRAEL (*without respect*). Aye, aye, sir. (*Goes aloft, skilled and confident.*)

The ship rolls and pitches in heavy seas.

SMOLLETT. All hands on deck! Haul sail, and batten down! Haul sail!

A bright flash of lightning, a crack of thunder.

SILVER (*to* JIM). Get below, boy, and hold on where you can!

The sound of roaring wind, and lashing sea and rain, as the storm breaks with savage fury. JIM *crosses the deck but is sent tumbling. It seems he must be swept overboard until* SILVER, *with great courage and strength, reaches out and pulls him to safety.* JIM *flings himself down and clings on for dear life. The storm continues to rage and blow.*

MR ARROW, *with a safety rope around his waist, crosses the deck against the teeth of the gale. The ship pitches and he's flung overboard, held only by the rope. He struggles to haul himself aboard.* ISRAEL, *climbing down from aloft, takes hold of the life-saving rope.*

ARROW. Pull me in, man! Pull me in!

ISRAEL *looks around to check that no one's watching, and then he takes out his knife. He takes the chance to show* MR ARROW *his knife, and his intention, before cutting the rope.* MR ARROW *vanishes overboard, swallowed in an instant by the storm.* ISRAEL *pulls himself to safety, and disappears into the hold. The storm abates.*

GRAY. Man overboard! Man overboard!

SMOLLETT. Who is it?

GRAY. Mr Arrow, sir. All present, save Mr Arrow.

LIVESEY. We must turn back for him!

SMOLLETT. He's long gone, in those seas. There's nothing to be done.

TRELAWNEY. May God take his soul.

SMOLLETT (*sharply*). Israel Hands!

ISRAEL (*alarmed at hearing his name*). Aye, sir.

SMOLLETT. Step forward. (ISRAEL *steps forward*.) I saw your work.

ISRAEL. You saw, sir?

SMOLLETT. Aye, I saw . . . How you went aloft and hauled sail. It was right well done. Without it we would have lost the mast. Now, the ship needs a first mate, if you will agree to it.

ISRAEL. I do, sir, much obliged to you.

SMOLLETT. Very well, Mr Hands. (*Announces to the* CREW.) Israel Hands is first mate. Return to your duties. The ship sails on!

The CREW *resume their work.* JIM *and* SILVER *serve food to* LIVESEY *and* TRELAWNEY – *a midday snack on deck.*

SILVER. A hot bite for you, gentlemen.

LIVESEY (*savouring the food*). I'll say it again, Silver, you're a marvel.

TRELAWNEY. A sorceror! These past weeks I've never eaten so well. I could almost wish to sail like this for ever.

SILVER. The boy's a great help, sir, and you've bought the best of rations – with double nips of grog, duff on odd days, and always a barrel of apples for anyone who wants.

TRELAWNEY. Russet reds, from my own orchard.

SMOLLETT. Spoiled foc'sle hands make devils, that's my belief! To work!

SILVER. Aye, sir!

SILVER and JIM *go.* SMOLLETT *walks away from* LIVESEY *and* TRELAWNEY, *inspecting the ship.*

TRELAWNEY. A trifle more of that man, and I shall explode!

JIM stands, gazing up at the mainmast, and the distant crow's nest. ISRAEL *approaches.*

ISRAEL. Come on, lad, time you took a climb.

JIM. No . . . Not now . . .

ISRAEL. No man can call himself a sailor till he's looked down on the world from the crow's nest . . . Up you go.

JIM *starts to climb, but freezes.*

JIM. I can't . . .

ISRAEL. Now, that ain't much good. Can't ain't no good to no one. I'm giving you an order! Get aloft, Hawkins. Aloft, I say!

SILVER. Leave him be. (ISRAEL *goes, laughing.* JIM *climbs down.*) Never you mind, now . . .

JIM. I'm ashamed, John.

SILVER. Ain't no reason for shame . . . Some can climb, and some can't, and there's an end to it . . . Come on and have a yarn with old John. Nobody more welcome than yourself, my son . . . Let's see what Her Majesty has to say . . . (*He uncovers a cage, opens it, and takes out his parrot,* FLINT.) So here you are, my beauty.

FLINT. Pieces of eight, pieces of eight!

SILVER. Shut your beak, you'll give me a headache.

JIM (*laughing*). What are pieces of eight?

SILVER. Golden coins, Jim, fabulous golden coins.

JIM (*gently stroking the parrot*). How old is she?

SILVER. Near two hundred years, I'd say, they lives for ever mostly, and if anyone's seen more wickedness, it must be the Devil himself. She's sailed with the great Cap'n England as well as Flint. She's been at Madagascar, Malabar, Surinam, Providence and Portobello. She was at the fishing up of the wrecked Plate ships. It's there she learned 'Pieces of eight', and little wonder, three hundred and fifty thousand of 'em there were! (*Strokes her, gives her a lump of sugar.*) She was at the boarding of the *Viceroy of the Indies*, she was, and to look at her, you'd think she was a babby. But you smelt powder, didn't you, Cap'n?

FLINT. Cut his throat, drink his blood. Cut his throat, drink his blood.

SILVER (*putting her back in cage, covers it*). Now, there's the pity, Jim . . . Treasure ships sail on seas of blood . . . You can't touch pitch, and not be mucked. And ain't it a shame, ain't it a shame? (*Ruffles* JIM's *hair, and goes.*)

The watch are all forward, looking for the island. JIM *joins* LIVESEY *and* TRELAWNEY *who both have their telescopes glued to their eyes.*

LIVESEY. If our calculations are right we should sight land within the hour.

TRELAWNEY (*as excited as a small boy*). I see it in my mind's eye, and then I look again and it's gone.

LIVESEY (*still searching the horizon*). Fetch me an apple, Jim, there's a lad.

They continue their watch. JIM *goes to the apple barrel, and reaches in.*

JIM. Empty . . . (*Peers in.*) Some at the bottom . . .

JIM leans in, but he can't reach far enough, and comes up empty-handed. He clambers up, and lowers himself down into the barrel. He begins to climb out with an apple in his hand. SILVER *approaches, talking to a young sailor,* DICK.

SILVER. You're young, you are, but as smart as paint. I seen that soon as I set eyes on you, and I'll talk to you like any man.

JIM (*to himself*). The words he first spoke to me . . .

His instincts alerted by this repetition, JIM *hides in the barrel.* SILVER *and* DICK *stand right up close to the barrel, with* SILVER *sometimes leaning on it to keep his balance.*

DICK (*admiringly*). So was you the Cap'n?

SILVER. No, not I. Flint was Cap'n. I was quartermaster. The same broadside I lost my leg, old Pew lost his daylights.

DICK. Where's all Flint's men now?

SILVER. Why most of them's aboard here, I seen to that.

DICK. Now, Silver, the way you talk, I feel a rope around my neck.

SILVER. I'll tell you about gentlemen of fortune. They lives rough, and they risk swinging, but they eat and drink like fighting cocks, and when a cruise is done, why it's hundreds of pounds in their pockets, and none o' yer measly pennies and farthings.

DICK. I like that, I won't lie, but I ain't cuttin' no throats.

SILVER. Then I'll put it to you different. (*His easy manner takes on a chillingly hard edge.*) Here it is, boyo. There was some that was feared of Pew, and Pew was feared of Flint, but Flint, well he was feared of one man alone – Long John Silver. Do you take my meaning?

DICK (*very frightened, struggling to hide it*). I'll tell you now, I didn't like this job till I had this talk, John. There's my hand on it. (*They shake hands.*)

ISRAEL *joins them, as silent as a shadow.*

SILVER. It's all right. Dick's square.

ISRAEL. Oh, he's no fool is Dick. He didn't want to go like Mr Arrow, did he? But here's what I want to know. When do we strike? I've had my fill of Captain Smollett. He's lorded it over me long enough! I want to go into his cabin, I do. I wants their pickles and fine wine . . . (*Fingers his knife.*) And I claims that boy Hawkins, with his eyes shinin' as if the world was made for him and him alone. I'll have his bones!

SILVER. You'll speak soft, and you'll keep sober, till I give the word!

ISRAEL *glares challengingly at* SILVER, *as if he means to fight, but he looks away, backing down.*

ISRAEL. Well, I don't say no, do I? What I says is when?

SILVER. The last moment I can manage, that's when! Here's a first-rate captain sails the ship for us. Here's this Squire and Doctor with a map and such. I don't know where it is, do I? I means them to help us find the gold, and get it aboard. Then we'll see. If I was sure of you all, I'd have Smollett navigate us halfway back before I struck.

DICK. We're all seamen, ain't we?

SILVER. Aye, we can steer a course, but who's to set one? But I know the sort you are. Hurry, hurry, hurry, you'll have your mouthful of rum tomorrow, and go hang . . . I'll finish with 'em at the island.

DICK. What will we do with 'em?

SILVER. Mark you here, I'm an easy gentleman, but dooty is dooty, so I gives my vote – death! When I'm in Parlyment, and riding in my coach, I don't want none o' them sea-lawyers in the cabin comin' home, unlooked for, like the Devil at prayers. Wait is what I say, but when the time comes, let her rip!

ISRAEL. John Silver, you're my man!

SILVER. Aye, and there's one thing I claim – Squire Trelawney! That fat farmer dressed up in admiral's rig like a pig at a party! I'll wring his pig's head off his body with these hands! Dick, jump up like a sweet lad, and get me an apple to wet my pipe like.

DICK. It's near empty.

SILVER. Then takes your knife, and stab down.

DICK pulls his knife, and prepares to stab down into the barrel.

LOOKOUT (*loud, from off*). Land ho! Land ho!

SILVER, ISRAEL and DICK rush forward. JIM, pale and riven, climbs out of the barrel.

JIM. It's a lie . . . Everything's a lie . . . (JIM *joins the excited crowd forward. He tries to attract the attention of* LIVESEY *and* TRELAWNEY.) Doctor, Doctor!

They're too excited to heed him.

LIVESEY. There's the island! Dead ahead!

TRELAWNEY. By my word, there's even gold in the light!

There is a golden glow to the light.

JIM. Doctor, please listen!

SILVER takes him by the arm, causing JIM to start with fright and pull away.

SILVER. Ah, you're excited, and why wouldn't you be? When you want to go exploring, you just ask old John.

He gives JIM a friendly clap on the shoulder, and moves away.

JIM (*to* LIVESEY). Please listen, you've got to!

DOCTOR. What is it?

JIM. I have terrible news . . . I must speak to the Captain, and the Squire! Please, Doctor!

LIVESEY picks up on JIM's urgency, and goes to speak privately in SMOLLETT's ear. SMOLLETT quickly takes the measure of things, and addresses the CREW.

SMOLLETT. So lads, we've sighted our destination. You've done your duty as I've never seen it done better. The Squire, the Doctor and I are going below to drink to your health and luck, and you'll have double rations to drink to the good Squire!

DICK. A cheer for Squire Trelawney!

The CREW give a rousing cheer, and go to take their rum. SMOLLETT, LIVESEY, TRELAWNEY and JIM talk in private.

TRELAWNEY. What a crew! What great lads!

JIM. No, sir, not so! They plan to kill us all, steal the treasure and take the ship! And Silver is leader . . . John Silver . . . The man I thought my best friend in all the world.

TRELAWNEY. Silver? It can't be true.

JIM. I hid in the apple barrel and heard them, Silver and Israel Hands and young Dick . . . All Flint's old crew are aboard, all of them!

TRELAWNEY. By heaven, I could find it in my heart to blow this ship to kingdom come! Captain, you were right and I was wrong. I own myself an ass, and I await your orders.

SMOLLETT. No more an ass than I who made mutiny his first mate. But we know what's what, thanks to you, Hawkins, and so here's how we'll play it. We can't turn back. If I gave the word to go about, they would rise at once. Instead I'll give an order they like – to take a boat and go ashore.

TRELAWNEY. That will split their number.

LIVESEY. Jim can help us more than anyone. The men are not shy with you, and you're a noticing lad. Jim, will you go ashore with these cut-throats?

JIM. I will, Doctor, and find out what more I can.

SMOLLETT. Brave lad. We'll stay aboard and take back the ship if we may. If they're too many, we'll row ashore to the stockade marked on the chart. There must be some faithful hands, we have guns, and we have the chart. We're not beat yet. Are we agreed?

ALL. Agreed.

TRELAWNEY. Hawkins, we put all our faith in you.

JIM. I'll do my best, sir . . .

SMOLLETT. We can ask no more than that. Good luck to you, Hawkins. Good luck to us all.

They rejoin the CREW.

My lads, we've had a long journey and a turn ashore'll hurt nobody. You can take a boat and as many as please go ashore for the afternoon.

The CREW *give a loud cheer.*

Mr Hands, lay off and drop anchor.

ISRAEL. Aye, aye, sir. (*Calls out.*) Haul sail and cast anchor! And ready the forward shoreboat!

SILVER (*with an edge*). Aye, Mr Hands.

JIM (*to* SILVER). Can I come with you, John?

SILVER. Wouldn't go without you, son. This is a sweet spot for any lad to get ashore on. You'll swim and climb trees, and hunt goats, you will. It makes me feel young again, and it's a fine thing to be young again, and have ten toes. (*Puts his arm around* JIM*'s shoulders.*) So come on you with me – to the island, the island of our dreams!

Scene Four

The island, steaming in the hot sun. The sound of waves and seabirds. The haunting calls and cries of unseen animals. Enter SILVER *with* GEORGE MERRY.

SILVER. George, you'll take care of Alan, I'll have a word with our Tom.

MERRY. It's done.

He goes. Enter TOM *and* JIM.

SILVER (*to* JIM). On you go! What are you waiting for? Run, play, explore! Get on with you – shoo, scat, vamoose!

JIM *runs off.*

Tom, mate, it's because I think gold dust of you, gold dust, that I gives you this warning.

JIM *returns, unseen by* SILVER *and* TOM, *and hides and watches.*

All's up, you can't make nor mend. It's to save your neck I'm havin' this talk, and if one o' the wild 'uns knew it, where'd I be then, Tom, tell me that? So – are you with us?

TOM. Silver, you're honest, or has the name for it, and you're brave, or I'm mistook. Will you be led away by this mess of swabs? Nay, not you. As sure as God sees me, I'd sooner lose my hand than turn against my dooty . . .

The sound of a distant scream of pain and terror which echoes in the rocks of Spyglass Hill.

In heaven's name, John, tell me what was that?

SILVER. That, mate? Oh, I reckon that'll be Alan.

TOM. Then rest his soul for a true seaman! And as for you, John Silver, long you've been a mate of mine, but you're mate of mine no more. If I die like a dog, I'll die in my dooty. You've killed Alan, have you? Kill me too, if you can. But I defies you!

He turns his back on SILVER, *and walks away. With a sudden movement* SILVER *strikes* TOM *in the back with his crutch, and is on him in a flash, slaying him instantly with his flashing blade.* JIM, *stunned and appalled, can't help but step forward out of hiding.*

JIM (*dazed*). You killed him . . . He was a good man, he turned his back on you, and you killed him . . .

SILVER (*pained, gently*). Now, that weren't no pretty sight for a lad t'see, and I'm sorry for it. That spyglass hilltop yonder, it'll be going round and round, topsy-turvy before your eyes . . .

JIM. You killed him . . .

SILVER. There'll be bells ringin', distant voices shouting in your ears. But I'll tell you no lie, it's just the way sometimes things has to go, and what you do, lad, is you moves on. We're friends, ain't we? Well, then, join with me, and I'll make you rich.

JIM (*quietly, to himself*). No . . .

Enter MERRY *and some other* PIRATES.

SILVER. Come on! What a pair we'll make. Together we'll be kings o' the world!

JIM. Never! I've seen the kind of friend you are! I say the same to you as that brave man you murdered – I defies you, John Silver, I defies you!

He flees into the forest.

SILVER. Get after him! Find him!

MERRY *and the* PIRATES *go after* JIM.

Find him, you dogs! Find him, and kill him!

End of Act One.

ACT TWO

Scene One

The island. Deep in the forest. Enter JIM, *exhausted from running in the steaming heat.*

JIM. Lost . . . No one could be more lost . . . I'll never see the Doctor again, the Squire . . . or my mother . . . I'm sorry, Mother, I wanted to make you rich, but I've found nothing . . . Nothing in the middle of nowhere . . .

A strange creature is glimpsed, moving quickly through the branches.

(*Terrified of the apparition.*) What was that? (*Picks up stick.*) Show yourself. I won't run any more. (*Brandishes stick.*) If it's a fight you want, here it is! Come on, I'm waiting!

A wild, ragged figure leaps out behind JIM, *causing him to yelp with fright, turn and lift his stick to strike, but before he can deliver a blow, the figure falls to his knees, holding out his clasped hands in supplication.* JIM *stares in amazement at a skinny beanpole of a man with long, wild, white hair and beard. He is clad in tatters of old ship's canvas held together by various incongruous fastenings of brass buttons, bits of stick and loops of tarry twine.*

Who . . . Who are you?

BEN GUNN. I'm Ben Gunn, I am. And who are you, I wonder? Oh, he's a dream sent to torment old Ben . . . Nothing but a dream, for sure. (*Touches* JIM's *sleeve cautiously, strokes his hand and face in wonder.*) Real! He's real! No, he's not . . . He is . . . He can't be . . .

JIM. Of course I'm real.

BEN GUNN. Beg pardon, I ain't spoke to a Christian these three years.

JIM. Three years!

BEN GUNN. Like heaven it is to hear another man's voice.

JIM. I'm Jim, Jim Hawkins. Were you shipwrecked?

BEN GUNN. Nay, marooned, I was, left here to die three years
  gone by, and lived on goats since, and berries and oysters. Wher-
  ever a man is, says I, a man can do for himself. But, mate, you
  mightn't have a piece of cheese about you, now, might you?
  (JIM *shakes his head*.) Pity . . . Many's the long night I've
  dreamed of cheese – toasted cheese, with pepper and pickle.

JIM. If ever I get aboard again, you'll have cheese by the ton.

BEN GUNN. If ever you get aboard? What's to stop you? (*Suddenly fearful*.) You tell me true, that ain't Flint's ship.

JIM. It's not his ship. Flint's dead, but his crew are here.

BEN GUNN. Not a man with one leg?

JIM. Aye, Silver.

BEN GUNN. If you're a friend of Long John, I'm dead meat and I
  knows it!

JIM. He's a murderer, and no friend of mine! There are good men
  who hope to stand against him.

BEN GUNN. Bein' good ain't no good against the likes of Silver.
  I'll tell you true, Jim, I was in Flint's ship when he buried the
  treasure. He went ashore with six men, killed them all so only he
  knew where the treasure was hid. He comes aboard – Billy
  Bones was the mate, Long John the quartermaster – and they
  asks him where the treasure was, and he just laughs in their
  faces, and says – 'You're welcome to look for it if you've got a
  lifetime to spare.'

JIM. Why did they leave you here?

BEN GUNN. It weren't them. I was in another ship three years
  back. 'Boys,' says I, 'there's Flint's island, let's land and find his
  treasure.' Twelve days they looked in the hot sun, till they'd had
  enough o' diggin' and my notions, and then they says – 'As for
  you, Ben Gunn, here's a musket and a spade. You can stay and
  find this fool's gold for yourself! We're off!' And they leaves me.
  Just like that, they leaves me.

JIM. You poor man.

BEN GUNN (*stung*). Poor? Poor? Don't you go thinkin' that! I may
  not look much, but this is my island. I'm king here, king! You
  tell that to those good men o' yours! (*As if talking to himself*.)

Don't shout, Ben . . . Makes me frightened . . . (*Proud again*.) I could have lain down and died, I could, but I fought to live. That tree there, that's where I killed my first goat. And I made myself a little round boat for fishing. I keeps it down there by that white rock – try her if you like, she won't sink . . . (*Holds his head*.) Can't stop talking . . . Been so long since I had anyone to talk to but the man in the moon . . . But I ain't poor, hear me, I'm rich, rich, 'cept I ain't got no cheese, and I'll make a man of you, Jim. You'll bless the stars, you will, you was the first that found me.

The sound of gunshot, the roar of a cannon, and distant shouts. JIM climbs to get a better view, and find his bearings.

JIM. The Doctor and the Squire are rowing for shore! They're firing the ship's cannon at them. (*The roar of a cannon*.) They're hit! They're swimming for shore.

BEN GUNN (*to himself*). Starting again . . . Killing, murdering, all the madness man brings with him . . .

JIM. They're on the beach. But Silver and his men are after them. No, it's a race . . . They're racing for the stockade!

BEN GUNN. Hate this, hate it, hate it . . . Best he'd never come . . . Never . . . (*Goes silently*.)

JIM. Come on, Ben, they need us . . . Ben? Where are you? (*Calls out*.) Help us, Ben! Please! Help us if you can.

Giving up on him, JIM runs off for the stockade.

Scene Two

The stockade. The sound of loud shouts and gunfire. SMOLLETT, LIVESEY, TRELAWNEY and GRAY, an honest seaman, weighed down with pistols and muskets strung over their backs, rush into the tumbledown stockade and immediately take desperate shelter behind its broken walls. Musketballs fly all around them, forcing them to duck and hide. They fire back at their unseen enemy. PIRATES appear, first at the door, and then a window. SMOLLETT shoots the first, GRAY the second. JIM climbs in a window and stands, frozen with fear and confusion.

LIVESEY. Down, Jim, down!

He throws JIM *to the ground.*

JIM (*seeing a* PIRATE *take aim at* LIVESEY*'s back*). Doctor!

TRELAWNEY *shoots the* PIRATE, *who falls back out the window. The four men take separate positions and fire on their attackers.*

SMOLLETT. They're on the run! Take as many as you can!

GRAY *and* LIVESEY *fire again. A scream of pain is heard. They maintain a keen watch outside, and reload muskets, as they talk.*

TRELAWNEY. That's two from the boat rowed after us, and four more here.

LIVESEY. They're six less, and we're one more. It's good to see you, Jim.

SMOLLETT. We thought you dead, Hawkins.

JIM. I ran for my life, but they killed Alan and Tom.

GRAY. Good men, both. They would never join Silver. God rest their souls.

LIVESEY. This is Abraham Gray. He took sides with us.

GRAY. I ain't no saint, but I'll do my duty to ship and Captain.

TRELAWNEY. And I thank you for it, with all my heart.

SMOLLETT. Even with Abraham we were still too few to take back the ship. (*Feeling it badly.*) I've never lost a ship.

LIVESEY. What else, Jim?

JIM. I met a castaway. He talked and talked, but all I made out was he has his own boat, and would do anything for cheese.

LIVESEY (*laughing*). Then he must be my servant, for I keep a lump of Parmesan cheese in my snuffbox.

A volley of shots pepper the stockade, but no one is hit.

TRELAWNEY. We're not lost yet. We have these walls, and if we hold out long enough they'll drink themselves to death.

LIVESEY. Aye, or swamp fever will kill 'em.

SMOLLETT (*darkly*). But they have the ship, gentlemen. They have the ship, and the ship is everything . . .

SILVER's voice is heard.

SILVER (*offstage*). Ahoy, there! Flag of truce!

SMOLLETT. Heads down, and muskets ready! Look lively!

SILVER appears outside the stockade, holding up a white flag.

SILVER (*insolently cheerful*). Cap'n Silver, sir, to come on board and talk terms.

TRELAWNEY. My heart, here's promotion.

SMOLLETT. Cap'n Silver? Don't know him? Who's he?

Whistling to himself, SILVER *comes into the compound.*

SILVER. The lads have chosen me Cap'n, after your desertion, sir.

SMOLLETT. On the ground, Silver, like the dog you are!

GRAY kicks away his crutch, forcing SILVER down to the ground.

GRAY. You heard Captain Smollett!

SILVER. That's enough, now, Abraham.

GRAY points his pistol at SILVER.

GRAY. Alan and Tom were friends of mine!

SMOLLETT. Hold your fire, that's an order!

GRAY puts away his pistol.

SILVER. And here's Jim. Good day to you, boy . . . And the good Doctor Livesey . . . Well, here we all are, a happy family . . .

SMOLLETT. If you have something to say, say it!

SILVER. Very well. Here it is – we wants that treasure, and we'll have it, that's our point. You wants to live, I reckon, and that's yours. You have a map, don't you?

SMOLLETT. That's as may be.

SILVER. Give us that map and we'll leave you food and supplies, and send the first ship we see to pick you up. Handsomer than that, you couldn't get.

SMOLLETT. Is that all?

SILVER. Every last word, by thunder! Refuse that, and you've seen the last of me but musketballs!

SMOLLETT. Very good. Now you'll hear me. If you come up unarmed, one by one, I'll agree to clap you all in irons and take you home to a fair trial. If you won't, I'll see you all to Davy Jones.

SILVER. Have a care, Smollett!

SMOLLETT. You can't find the treasure, you can't sail the ship, and you can't kill us behind these walls! In the name of heaven, I'll put a bullet in your back when next I meet you! So tramp, my lad! Bundle out of this place, hand over hand, you dog, and double quick!

Stunned and furious, SILVER *attempts to stand.*

SILVER. Give me a hand up!

TRELAWNEY. Not I!

SILVER. Who'll give me a hand up?

JIM *steps forward, but* LIVESEY *holds him back.*

LIVESEY. Save your pity for those who deserve it.

SILVER *crawls to his crutch, uses it to haul himself upright.*

SILVER (*spits*). That's what I think of ye! Gentlemen you call your-selves! You've more greed for gold than any poor sailor I ever seen! Before the hour's up I'll stove in this old blockhouse! Laugh, by thunder, laugh! Before I'm done you'll laugh on the other side. Them that dies'll be the lucky ones!

SILVER *stumbles off, cursing.*

SMOLLETT. So, lads, I gave Silver a broadside. I pitched it in red-hot to make him angry, make him attack before we run short of food and water. We're outnumbered, but we fight in shelter, and we fight with discipline. Load all pistols and muskets. Keep your blades ready. Hawkins, stay down, and load our guns quick as you can. (*Hands him a pistol.*) This is yours. Remember you have only one shot. If you have to use it, get as close as you can, like this, then let fire.

They take up their positions with pistols and muskets at the ready.

JIM (*as they wait for the attack*). Captain Smollett?

SMOLLETT. What is it?

JIM. You said the ship was everything. The wild man I met, Ben Gunn, he has a little boat. One of us could row out to the *Hispaniola* and take her back.

SMOLLETT. In your dreams, lad.

TRELAWNEY. Think first of staying alive, for here they come.

SMOLLETT. Hold your fire. Wait till you can smell 'em . . . Wait . . . Wait, lads . . . Fire!

A cloud of PIRATES attack in a chaos of shots, and screams of rage and pain. It all happens so fast that JIM barely has time to load one musket, but the defenders of the stockade fire with discipline and accuracy. Even so, a number of PIRATES threaten to breach the walls. LIVESEY shoots and misses, and engages in a cutlass fight with a PIRATE who has leapt onto a window ledge. Another PIRATE confronts JIM who takes aim with his pistol, but he can't bring himself to fire. GRAY saves JIM by shooting the PIRATE who tumbles and vanishes behind the wall. SMOLLETT is hit in the shoulder, but fights on. LIVESEY gets the better of his opponent, wounding him, and forcing him to flee.

TRELAWNEY. They're on the run!

They cheer their victory and survival with savage fury.

GRAY (*brandishing his cutlass*). Run, you curs! Run like the beaten dogs you are!

He is hit in the chest, and sent stumbling to the ground.

LIVESEY. Abraham! (*He rushes to his side.*)

GRAY. We gave them a beating, didn't we, Doctor?

LIVESEY (*gently, knowing he's dying*). Yes, we did, Abraham . . .

GRAY. No one can say Abraham Gray ran from a fight . . .

SMOLLETT. No one will ever say that.

GRAY. Am I going, Doctor?

LIVESEY. Don't you worry . . . You're going home, Abraham . . . You're going home . . .

GRAY *dies.*

JIM (*holding back tears of anger and hurt*). No! He can't be . . . He can't be dead! He was brave and good. He didn't deserve to die.

Mr Arrow and Alan and Tom, and now him. How can they be dead when others who rob and lie and kill are still alive?

SMOLLETT (*as* LIVESEY *tends to his wound*). No one can answer that, Jim.

TRELAWNEY. That's God's business.

JIM. No, it's our business! We came here! We made it happen, no one else!

LIVESEY. Jim . . .

JIM. Can't just wait here and watch people die one by one . . . That's just stupid . . . We started it, and we can end it . . . We can end it!

He runs out of the stockade.

LIVESEY. Jim, come back! They'll kill you! Come back!

TRELAWNEY. I'll go after him.

SMOLLETT (*in pain from his wound*). Leave him be, man! The boy doesn't have the stomach for a fight. He's a coward who won't obey orders, a coward who runs. We're better off without him. Let him go.

Scene Three

The deck of the Hispaniola. *Night. Bright moonlight.* ISRAEL, *left in charge of the ship, paces on the deck. He wears one of* TRELAWNEY*'s silk shirts, and one of* SMOLLETT*'s captain's jackets worn loose over it. He drinks from a bottle of stolen wine. He sings to himself.*

ISRAEL.
But one man of her crew alive
What put to sea with twenty five . . .

If I was Captain . . . No 'if' about it, by thunder . . . *When* I'm Captain . . . (*He issues commands to an imaginary crew.*) You there, get aloft and haul sail or I'll have the skin off your back! Load the cannon! Fire, you damned dogs! Kill them! Kill them all! We sail for the land where mountains are made of gold and rivers flow with rum! And you sail under the command of Israel

Hands, Captain of the *Hispaniola*, and pirate chief of all the seven seas! (*The ship heaves suddenly, causing* ISRAEL *to stumble and curse*.) Anchor's cut! What dog dares to . . . (JIM *climbs aboard*.) You!

JIM. I've come aboard to take possession of the ship, Mr Hands. You'll regard me as your captain until further notice.

ISRAEL. Captain, be damned! You've cut her loose. She's flying before the wind. You'll break her on the rocks!

JIM. Not if we steer her.

ISRAEL (*contemptuously*). Steer her where?

JIM. Round the headland onto the sands of the north inlet. We'll beach her where no one'll see her. Well, Mr Hands, what's it to be? Take her to safety, or onto the rocks? Lose the ship and we'll be here for ever . . .

With a curse, ISRAEL *leaps into action, taking the wheel and struggling to steer the flying ship.*

I won't have these colours. I'll strike 'em, by heaven! (*He hauls down the black pirate flag, and throws it overboard*.) God save the King, and there's an end to Cap'n Silver!

ISRAEL. Hand me a bottle.

JIM. Which one?

ISRAEL. One that ain't empty! (JIM *hands him a bottle*.) Good lad. (*With a grain of derision*.) So you've got the better of us. I've tried my fling and lost, and it's you has the wind of me. Here we are, on course for the north inlet. You've some cheek, I'll say that. Here, boy, hold the wheel till I lash that sail.

JIM takes the wheel. ISRAEL *goes behind him.*

Feels, good, don't it?

JIM (*exhilarated*). It feels wonderful.

ISRAEL. Flies like a bird she does . . . And once she's beached, you just needs to take a line ashore at low water, and take a rope about one o' them big pines. Come high water, off she'll come as sweet as natur'. You're a born seaman, no doubt, it's in yer blood . . .

Alerted by this excessive flattery, JIM *turns just in time to escape* ISRAEL's *flashing blade. He stumbles backwards, taking out his pistol and aiming it at* ISRAEL.

JIM. Stay back or I'll fire!

ISRAEL. Then fire, you swab! Come on! You can't, can you? It takes a man's hand to pull that trigger, an' you ain't no man! (JIM *pulls the trigger, but it misfires*.) Misfired, you dog! You let seawater in, you babby. You'll die for that. I'll have your bones!

He charges like a bull. JIM *runs like a sheep before his butcher.* ISRAEL *slashes with his knife as they dodge and feint, eyeing each other desperately. Just as it seems* ISRAEL *has* JIM *at his mercy, the ship strikes the sand and they both roll and tumble across the deck.* JIM *is first to his feet. He struggles to dry and reprime his pistol.*

We've hit the sand . . . Ship's safe, but it's the end for you, mate.

JIM. You don't have to kill me.

ISRAEL. Why not, tell me?

JIM. You've lived in lies and blood all your life. For God's mercy, it's time to stop.

ISRAEL. For thirty years I've sailed the seas and I've never seen good come o' goodness yet! Him as strikes first is my fancy, dead men don't bite. Them's my views, amen, and so be it!

He lunges at JIM, *who jumps up onto a railing and begins to climb.* ISRAEL *begins to laugh.*

But you can't climb, can you? You're too feared to climb . . .

But JIM *keeps climbing, until he stops at a crosstrees, and tries to dry his pistol.*

You're shaking, ain't you, shakin' fit to fall . . . Time we put an end to this.

ISRAEL *begins to climb quickly and effortlessly.*

JIM. Stay back.

ISRAEL. I'll have you!

JIM (*aiming his pistol*). I'm warning you. Dead men don't bite!

ISRAEL (*climbing ever closer*). I'll cut you, boy, I'll cut out your heart!

JIM fires. This time there is no misfire, and ISRAEL, shot from point blank range, falls overboard.

JIM (*both triumphant and sick to his heart*). I've killed him . . . Killed him . . . (*Climbs down, peers over the side.*) There he lies on the white sand under the shallow water . . . (*Starts with terror.*) He moves, he moves! No, it's only the current moves him . . . (*Steps back onto the deck, touches the wheel.*) I've taken you back and hidden you. Now you wait ready for true men to board you and get to sea again . . . Back now, to fight with my friends . . . I'll keep the double peaks behind me and Spyglass Hill on my right . . . Even the moon rises to light my way . . . Even the moon . . .

He goes.

Scene Four

The stockade. Night-time, towards dawn. The faint flicker of dying firelight. The sound of light snoring. JIM enters, stumbles over a sleeping figure.

VOICE. Who goes?

JIM. Doctor? Captain Smollett?

JIM is seized by a shadowy figure.

SILVER. Fetch a light!

TOM MORGAN and MERRY light brands from the smouldering fire. JIM is held by JOB ANDERSON. DICK holds a knife to JIM's throat.

ANDERSON. It's the brat!

JIM. Let go of me! Let go!

SILVER. So here's Jim Hawkins, dropped in like, eh? I take that friendly, so I do. Put him down, lads.

ANDERSON throws JIM down. He sits up, trapped against a wall.

JIM. Where are my friends?

SILVER. Not here, as you can see. It was the middle of the night when down comes Doctor Livesey with a flag of truce. 'Silver, you're sold out, the ship's gone,' he says. None of us had looked out, but we looked then and, by thunder, it was gone! Near stopped our hearts, that did. 'Let's bargain,' says the Doctor, and here we are – stores, brandy, blockhouse, firewood, and all they got was to live another day.

JIM. They're not dead . . . Thank God for it.

MERRY. But they ain't no friends of yours, no sir. Smollett, he says, 'As for that boy, I don't know where he's run, and I don't care.'

SILVER. He has you marked for a deserter, so you can't go back to your lot, can you? They won't have you. You've but one course to sail – you'll have to jine with Cap'n Silver.

JIM. Never.

SILVER. You'll have to, mate. I've always liked you for a lad of spirit, and the picter of my own self when I was young and free.

Rage and pride and sadness burn inside JIM.

JIM. Here's a thing or two I'll tell you – you're in a bad way, Silver, ship lost, treasure lost, men lost, your whole business gone to wreck and, if you want to know who did it, it was I! I was in the apple barrel and I heard you, and Dick Johnson, and Israel Hands, who's now at the bottom of the sea, and I told every word to the Captain so he knew your plan. And as for the ship, it was I who cut her anchor, and it was I killed Hands, and I who sailed the ship where you'll never find her! I no more fear you than I fear a fly, so kill me if you want, but I'll say one thing – spare me, and when you're in court for piracy, I'll save you all I can.

MORGAN. Damned upstart! It was him that knowed Black Dog.

MERRY. Aye, and it was this same boy that faked the chart from Billy Bones. First and last, we've split upon Jim Hawkins!

ANDERSON. Kill the brat!

MERRY. Aye, cut his mewlin' throat!

JIM. I'm not frightened, I won't be frightened! But I'll take it kindly if you tell the Doctor and the Captain the way I took it.

SILVER (*moved by* JIM*'s courage*). I'll bear it in mind.

ANDERSON *and* MORGAN *pull out their knives and advance on* JIM*, but conflicting feelings burn and erupt in* SILVER.

Avast there, you dogs! Maybe you thought you was Cap'n. By the powers, I'll teach you better! Take a cutlass, him that dares, and I'll see the colour of his insides! I'm Cap'n here, and I'm Cap'n because I'm the best man by a long sea-mile. If you won't fight me, then you'll obey! I like this boy. I never seen a better boy than that. He's more a man than any pair o' rats in this hole, so let me see who'll lay a hand on him!

MORGAN, MERRY, ANDERSON *and* DICK *form a huddle, and whisper conspiringly.*

You seem to have a lot to say. Pipe up and let me hear it!

MERRY. I'll be hanged if I'll be ruled by you, John Silver! We claims our right to step outside for a council of war!

SILVER. Step away, step away!

MORGAN, MERRY, ANDERSON *and* DICK *go outside.*

Now, look you here, Jim Hawkins, you're within half a plank of torture and death, but I stand by you through thick and thin. I didn't mean to, no, not till you spoke up all brave like, but I says to myself – you stand by Hawkins and Hawkins'll stand by you. You're his last card and, by heaven, John Silver, he's yours. I'll save your neck, and that way you can speak up, and save Long John from hanging. What do you say?

JIM. What choice do I have?

SILVER. None, same as me. That's why we can trust each other.

JIM. What I can do, I'll do.

SILVER. So we're together, then? Back to back?

SILVER *offers his hand.*

JIM. Back to back. You have my word, but I won't shake hands with you.

SILVER. Then it's a bargain! You speak up plucky and, by heaven, I've a chance! But first, the treasure . . . Only one thing bothers me. Why did the Doctor give up the map so easy? There's something under that – something surely under that . . .

Dawn breaks as ANDERSON, MORGAN, MERRY *and* DICK *come back in.* MERRY *steps forward, holding his closed right hand in front of him.*

Step up, I won't eat you. Hand it over. I know the rules. I won't hurt a depytation.

MERRY *slips something into* SILVER'*s hand, and hurries back to his companions.* SILVER *opens his hand, and looks at what he has been given.*

The Black Spot! Now here's an ugly sight. But where might you have got the paper? (*Examines it closely.*) Why, hillo, look here, now! This ain't lucky! You've cut this out of a Bible. What fool's cut a Bible?

MORGAN. There, what did I say? No good'll come of that, I said.

ANDERSON. It was Dick cut the Bible.

DICK (*uncomfortable*). Was all we had.

SILVER. Dick, was it? Then Dick can get to prayers. This spot is likely to hurt the giver more than the receiver.

ANDERSON. Belay that talk, John Silver!

MERRY. You've made a hash of this cruise. We've had enough of your bungling, and now you're friends with this boy.

SILVER. A hash, is it? Bungling? I'll give you answer to that, mate! One – if you'd listened to me we'd be in the ship with the treasure in the hold, and all we'd have to do is strike with England in our sights! Two – I spared Livesey so you can have a real college doctor to look after your wounds and fevers! What good's a dead doctor? Three – I spared this boy so we can bargain with him as a hostage! What good's a dead hostage? Four – you wonder why I parlayed with the Doctor. (*Takes out the map, throws it on the ground.*) There's why, you dogs!

MERRY. The map!

They leap on it like cats upon a mouse.

SILVER. Who's the better man now, George Merry? You can be Cap'n if you like. I resign! I'm done with it!

ANDERSON. No, Silver, stay!

DICK. I'm your man, John!

MORGAN. Silver's Cap'n, once and for all!

SILVER. So, George, I reckon you'll have to wait for another day.

A voice is heard.

VOICE. Blockhouse, ahoy!

Enter LIVESEY.

SILVER. Top o' the morning to you, Doctor. Come to look over your patients, have you?

ANDERSON. Dick don't feel well.

LIVESEY (*to* DICK). Open wide. (*Looks in his mouth.*) Tongue's black enough to frighten the French. He has swamp fever.

MORGAN. That's what comes from spoilin' Bibles!

SILVER. We've quite a surprise for you, a noo boarder and lodger.

LIVESEY (*seeing* JIM). Not Jim!

SILVER. The same Jim as ever was.

LIVESEY. So you have joined them.

JIM. No!

LIVESEY. I would never have believed it.

SILVER. You should have a word with the boy in private, sir.

ANDERSON. No! He'll run for it!

SILVER. Silence! The Doctor must understand he's a hostage, and not an enemy. (*To* JIM.) Do I have your word not to slip the cable?

JIM. You have it.

SILVER. Then we'll leave you to talk.

His CREW *complain.*

That's an order!

They leave reluctantly.

The boy'll tell you how I saved his life so you'll speak me fair and give me hope o' a drop of mercy.

LIVESEY. Why, John, you're not afraid?

SILVER. I'm no coward, but I've the shakes upon me for the gallows. First I spared you, and now the boy, and I trust you'll remember my good deeds above the bad.

LIVESEY. I won't forget.

SILVER. Then I'll let you talk.

He withdraws to the edge of earshot.

LIVESEY (*to* JIM, *accusingly*). Not an enemy?

JIM. No, sir, never!

LIVESEY. Why did you run? We'd lost a man, the Captain was hurt. It was a coward's act.

JIM. I wanted to end what we had started . . . I took back the ship.

LIVESEY. The ship?

JIM. I beached her in the north inlet. There she waits for when we need her . . . I killed Israel Hands.

LIVESEY. Killed him? Can you forgive me, Jim, forgive us all? Every step, it's you that saves our lives. You found out their plot, you took back the ship, and it was you found the wild man of the island – the best deed ever you did . . . But we can't stay here. Jump quick, and we'll run.

JIM. I gave my word.

LIVESEY. Let the shame be mine. Quick, now, run!

JIM. I won't break my word.

LIVESEY. They might kill Silver, torture you for the ship!

JIM. All the same, here I stay . . .

SILVER (*approaching*). It's time, Jim. They've caught the scent of gold.

LIVESEY. Don't be in any hurry after that treasure.

SILVER. I can only save my life and the boy's by finding Flint's gold.

LIVESEY. Then look out for trouble when you find it.

SILVER. Say what you mean!

LIVESEY. I'll say only this – keep the boy close beside you, and shout if you need help. (*He goes.*)

SILVER. Somethin' under his words I don't like . . . But that's one I owe you . . . I seen him wavin' you to run for it, and I seen you say no.

Enter ANDERSON, MERRY, DICK and MORGAN carrying picks and shovels, with muskets slung over their backs.

ANDERSON. Move, if you want to see gold!

MERRY (*brandishing map*). We'll find the treasure, and then this brat'll take us to the ship.

SILVER. That's what we'll do, lads. Luck's turnin' our way. (*Tying rope around JIM's waist.*) I'll keep him close, in case he thinks of running. We've lost good men, but that's more for us that lives! On then – to freedom and gold!

PIRATES. Freedom and gold!

Scene Five

The island. MERRY, ANDERSON *and* MORGAN *lead the way, followed by* DICK, *and then* SILVER *who leads* JIM *on a rope.*

MERRY (*reading map*). Skeleton Island east-south-east, and by east . . . Twenty paces north of tall tree . . .

MORGAN. What damned tree?

ANDERSON. It don't add up. Where do we take a bearing?

DICK gives a cry of alarm, examines something hidden in the ground.

MERRY. What is it?

DICK. Dead man's bones . . . Skeleton's all grown over with grass 'n creepers . . . Ain't a thing left, not a copper, or a knife or a baccy box . . .

SILVER. What sort of way is that for bones to lie? Arm stretched out that way . . . T'ain't in nature.

MERRY. Them's long bones, and the hair's been yellow.

ANDERSON. It's Allardyce . . . You remember the dog . . .

MORGAN. Aye, he went ashore with Flint. Flint killed all six came ashore with him.

DICK. Ain't good luck that . . . We're six, ain't we?

ANDERSON (*with a shiver*). If any spirit walked this island it would be Flint's. He died bad did Flint, ragin' and hollerin' for rum, and singin' that damned song . . .

A voice comes from the trees.

VOICE.
    Fifteen men on the dead man's chest
    Yo-ho-ho and a bottle of rum . . .

ANDERSON. It's him, it's Flint!

MORGAN. It's his spirit! He walks, he walks!

VOICE. Darby McGraw, Darby McGraw, fetch the rum, Darby McGraw!

MORGAN. It's him, I knows it! He's guarding the gold!

SILVER. Steady, lads. I'm here to get that treasure, and I'll not be beat by man nor devil. I never was feared of Flint when he was alive and, by the powers, I'll face him dead.

VOICE. Belay there, Silver. Don't you cross a spirit!

SILVER. There was an echo. Now, no man ever seen a spirit with a shadow, well then, what's he doing with an echo? Flesh and blood, I say!

MERRY. I'm wi' you, John. It was like Flint's voice, but it was liker someone else's, it was liker . . .

SILVER. Ben Gunn!

MORGAN. Aye, Ben Gunn it were!

ANDERSON. Nobody minds Ben Gunn, dead or alive, nobody minds him.

SILVER (*returning to the skeleton*). I've taken a notion, lads. These bones are Flint's compass. There's the point o' Skeleton Island stickin' up like a tooth. Just take a bearing, will you, along the lines o' them bones?

MORGAN. East-south-east by east! That's it!

SILVER. Follow Flint's compass to the tall tree, then twenty paces north, and we're rich men!

MERRY. I'll drink to that!

ANDERSON, MORGAN, MERRY and DICK rush off. SILVER goes to follow, but JIM holds him back by hauling on the rope.

JIM. When we find it, you won't forget our bargain?

SILVER. You'll soon see, won't you, mate? You'll soon see.

Consumed by greed for gold, SILVER pulls JIM off in pursuit of the PIRATES.

Enter MORGAN followed by ANDERSON, MERRY and DICK.

MORGAN (*pacing out*). Thirteen, fourteen, fifteen . . .

ANDERSON (*rushing ahead*). There's nothin'!

Enter SILVER and JIM.

MERRY. Just a hole in the ground! Boxes are broke! (*Holding up some pieces of rotten wood.*) Empty!

DICK. Someone's been here afore us!

They scrabble through the dirt like pigs through muck. SILVER hands JIM a pistol.

SILVER. Take that and stand by for trouble.

JIM. Back to back?

SILVER. Back to back.

MORGAN. It's gone, there's not a penny left!

ANDERSON. Just dirt, nothin' but dirt!

MERRY (*rounding savagely on SILVER*). Where's your treasure now? You're the man for plans, ain't you? You're him, the great man that never bungled nothing!

SILVER (*with the coolest insolence*). Dig away, boys. You're sure to find some pig-nuts.

ANDERSON. Pig-nuts!

MERRY. Mates, do you hear that? I tell you now, he's playing some game with us. Look in the face of him, and you'll see it wrote there!

SILVER. Ah, George Merry, standing for Cap'n again? You're a pushing lad, to be sure.

MERRY. There's only the two of them, mates. (*Pulling out his pistol and knife.*) One's the old cripple that's blundered us down to this, the other's that cub I mean to have the heart of! Now, mates!

They raise their pistols but three musket shots flash from the trees, and MERRY *falls.* ANDERSON, MORGAN *and* DICK *flee.* LIVESEY, TRELAWNEY, BEN GUNN *and* SMOLLETT, *with his arm in a ragged and bloody sling, come out of hiding.*

JIM. Doctor! Squire Trelawney!

SILVER. Ben Gunn, it is you.

BEN GUNN. How do, Silver? Pretty well, I thank ye, says you.

SILVER. Ben Gunn, to think it's you that's done me.

MERRY is raising his pistol, aiming it at JIM.

SMOLLETT (*shouting a warning*). Hawkins!

SILVER shoots MERRY dead.

SILVER. Reckon I settled you, George Merry.

TRELAWNEY (*with a hatred rooted in his own feelings of guilt*). You're the very Devil, Silver! Friend or foe, it makes no difference who you murder.

SILVER (*lightly, contemptuously*). That's about it, Squire, aye, I've a savage heart.

With a smile SILVER offers up his pistol. TRELAWNEY takes it, along with his other weapons.

SMOLLETT. Well then, Hawkins, you took back the ship.

JIM. Aye, sir, she's beached in the north inlet.

SMOLLETT. I've seen some brave deeds, but that's the bravest I ever heard. And to think I called you a coward. How can I ever thank you?

JIM. The treasure, sir. Tell me about the treasure.

LIVESEY. I followed your lead, Jim, and went to find Ben. He'd found the treasure a year ago. I asked him where he'd hid it . . .

BEN GUNN. All he had to do was give me a piece of cheese.

JIM. Where did you hide it?

BEN GUNN. Why, in full view. I carried it up to the mouth of yon high cave so it can catch the sun and glow like a beacon. I hoped a ship would see it and rescue me . . . Any minute now when the sun hits it, the fire'll be lit . . . You watch now. (*They are bathed in a golden light.*) There's your gold, my very own lighthouse.

TRELAWNEY. By my soul! The same light as that first day!

LIVESEY. It was right in front of our eyes!

SMOLLETT. So then, gentlemen, we'll load the ship and set sail for England.

SILVER. John Silver reporting for duty, sir.

TRELAWNEY. You dog! I never did blab, did I? I may have got drunk, but I didn't blab. You knew about the treasure all along.

SILVER. Ah now, that would be tellin'.

TRELAWNEY. You're a liar and imposter, sir! Dead men hang about your neck like millstones!

SILVER (*knuckling his brow insolently*). Yours and mine, both, thank you kindly, sir.

TRELAWNEY. You dare to thank me! I'll see you hang!

JIM. I gave my word to save him.

TRELAWNEY. I gave no such oath! He sails home in irons. He'll hang as a mutineer in Bristol Docks! The birds will pick his bones! Look lively, you dog, or I'll shoot you where you stand!

SILVER *begins to sing.*

SILVER.
Fifteen men on the dead man's chest –
You-ho-ho and a bottle of rum!
Drink and the Devil have done for the rest . . .

He continues to sing as they lead him off.

Scene Six

The beach of the north inlet. ANDERSON, MORGAN *and* DICK, *who shivers with fever, call out to those aboard the* Hispaniola.

ANDERSON. Ahoy there! Take us aboard!

DICK. Don't leave us here!

MORGAN (*to his companions*). They've hoist the sails, by heaven!

ANDERSON. You needs us! You needs us to crew the ship!

DICK (*to his companions*). Over there, look, they've left us stores.

MORGAN. They're plannin' to maroon us! (*Calling out to ship.*) Mercy of God, take us with you!

They fall to their knees with their hands raised in supplication.

ANDERSON. We're beggin' you to take us!

MORGAN. Don't leave us, please don't leave us here!

DICK. We'll swear an oath to ship and Captain!

MORGAN. We'll give no trouble!

ANDERSON. By my life and my soul we'll do our dooty!

DICK. Come back!

MORGAN. We're beggin' you, come back!

ANDERSON (*suddenly possessed by a violent rage*). I'll find you! One day I will, and that day'll be your last, you have my word on that!

DICK. I'll hunt you down! I'll cut your throats!

MORGAN. I'll have your blood! Hear me, you dogs, I'll have your bones!

They take out their pistols and fire after the ship. Light fades on them as they beg and curse and shout.

Scene Seven

The deck of the Hispaniola *moored in the harbour of an island port. The midday sun pours down its light like a blessing.* SILVER *is chained to the mast.* BEN GUNN *stands guard over him.*

BEN GUNN (*gazing at the shore*). So many people . . . Seein' a harbour again so busy-like . . . All the faces, they makes me dizzy. And those pearl divers, they stay under the water a lifetime and more . . .

Enter JIM, *carrying* SILVER*'s parrot in a cage.*

JIM. The Doctor's gone ashore for medical supplies, the Squire and the Cap'n'll take on stores and a new crew. In the morning we sail for England.

SILVER. Aye, and a rope round my neck.

BEN GUNN. Never thought I'd see you afraid, John Silver.

SILVER. It's not the rope I fear, it's being the entertainment for a gazin', gapin' multitude.

JIM sets down the cage, takes out a key and unlocks SILVER*'s chain.*

BEN GUNN. What are you doin'?

JIM. I gave my word to save him if I could.

BEN GUNN. You can't! The Squire wants different, boy, and you knows it.

JIM. I'll bear his anger. (*To* SILVER.) You're free to go. (*Hands him the cage.*) There are divers' boats selling fruit and flowers. One of them will take you ashore.

SILVER. That's right thoughtful of you, and how am I to pay my way?

JIM tosses him a small sack of gold. SILVER *looks inside it.*

Gold!

JIM. Our bargain's done. If I hear a whisper of you in England I'll see you hang.

SILVER. That's fair, I reckon, and I thank you for it. You're a good boy, Jim Hawkins, not that you'll care much for my opinion . . .

A fine boy . . . We'll never see each other again . . . You'll think of me as a friend, I hope . . .

SILVER *offers his hand.*

JIM. You're no friend of mine. Begone, John Silver, now and for ever.

SILVER. Ah, you that's young . . . You and me might have done a power of good together. Had you been my son, I'd have been a proud man, the proudest of men . . .

JIM. On your way!

SILVER. So it's farewell to you, Ben Gunn, and to you, Jim Hawkins . . . Good luck to you . . . Good luck . . .

He takes up his parrot, singing cheerfully and without self-pity as he goes.

Sing me a song of a lad that is gone,
Say could that lad be I?
Merry of soul he sailed on a day
Over the seas so high.
Give me again all that was there,
Give me the sun that shone.
Give me the eyes, give me the soul,
Give me the lad that's gone.

BEN GUNN. He's not a man you forget easy . . . Ever since I first knowed him he's never been far from my dreams.

JIM (*firmly, angry at the tears in his eyes*). We'll not talk of him!

BEN GUNN. As you say, sir.

JIM. Tell me, Ben, what will you do with your share?

BEN GUNN. Who knows? Open a cheese shop. (*Laughs.*) Nay, if I'm rich on Monday, I'm poor by Tuesday, that's my way. I'll spend it till it's gone . . . What about you?

JIM. I'll see my mother never needs for anything . . . Then maybe I think I'll buy a ship . . . My own ship, and sail all the oceans and seas of the wide world . . .

Music can be heard, the music a diver may hear in his dream when he finds the most perfect pearl of all. BEN GUNN takes a necklace of shells from around his neck.

BEN GUNN. I give thanks for the day I met you. It's an honour to know you, mate, and to sail with you . . . The greatest honour of my life . . . For the rest of my days I'll tell the tale of how I knew Jim Hawkins, the very Jim Hawkins that took on the pirates and saved his ship. No one who hears it will ever forget it.

Gravely, and with respect, he places the necklace around JIM's *neck.*

JIM. What's this, Ben? What does it mean?

BEN GUNN. You're a man now, Jim Hawkins, that's what it means . . . You're a man . . .

The End.